BFI Modern Classics

Rob White
Series Editor

Advancing into its second century, the cinema is now a mature art form with an established list of classics. But contemporary cinema is so subject to every shift in fashion regarding aesthetics, morals and ideas that judgments on the true worth of recent films are liable to be risky and controversial; yet they are essential if we want to know where the cinema is going and what it can achieve.

As part of the British Film Institute's commitment to the promotion and evaluation of contemporary cinema, and in conjunction with the influential BFI Film Classics series, BFI Modern Classics is a series of books devoted to individual films of recent years. Distinguished film critics, scholars and novelists explore the production and reception of their chosen films in the context of an argument about the film's importance. Insightful, considered, often impassioned, these elegant, beautifully illustrated books will set the agenda for debates about what matters in modern cinema.

Caravaggio

**Leo Bersani &
Ulysse Dutoit**

bfi Publishing

First published in 1999 by the
British Film Institute
21 Stephen Street, London W1P 2LN

The British Film Institute is the UK national
agency with responsibility for encouraging
the arts of film and television and conserving
them in the national interest.

Series design by Andrew Barron &
Collis Clements Associates

Typeset in Italian Garamond and Swiss 721BT
by D R Bungay Associates, Burghfield, Berks

Printed in Great Britain by
Norwich Colour Print, Drayton, Norfolk

British Library Cataloguing-in-Publication Data
A catalogue record for this book is available
from the British Library
ISBN 0-85170-724-6

Contents

Derek Jarman's *Caravaggio*

I

What did Derek Jarman learn from Caravaggio? There is no easy answer to this question (if indeed it can be answered at all), and it is not the same as asking why Jarman was attracted to Caravaggio. Jarman himself helps us to answer *that* question, and the account of his interest in the Italian painter is straightforward and persuasive. It seems to have been almost entirely a matter of self-recognition. As a painter and film-maker, Jarman saw in Caravaggio his own dominant aesthetic interests. Caravaggio painted, but, Jarman claims in the autobiographical text *Dancing Ledge*, 'had Caravaggio been reincarnated in this century it would have been as a film-maker, Pasolini'. Not just any film-maker, but the Italian homosexual painter/film-maker Pier Paolo Pasolini. Pasolini 'painted very badly', but that was perhaps a symptom of the times: 'Painting has degenerated into an obscure, hermetic practice, performed by initiates behind closed doors. There is a remarkable lack of emotional force in modern painting.' You can't 'shed a tear' for painting now, 'but you *can* weep at Pasolini's *Gospel According to Matthew,* and *Ricotta* can make you laugh. In 1600, who knows, painting might have evoked the same immediate response.'[1] Today only film has the power that painting may have had in Caravaggio's time.

The relation between film and power will be a central motif in our discussion of Jarman's work. For the moment, let's simply note that Pasolini is at least in part a stand-in for Jarman himself. Since Pasolini's 'emotional force' is something Jarman clearly sought to achieve in his own films, we might say that a reincarnated Caravaggio could just as well be Derek Jarman as Pier Paolo Pasolini. For Jarman, it is even as if Caravaggio were already working in a medium that hadn't yet been created. He writes that the latter 'had "invented" cinematic light' – by which he probably means that the sharply delineated lighting of Caravaggio's dark interiors creates the same effect as studio (as distinguished from outdoor) lighting in films. Caravaggio's treatment of

Biblical subjects is also congenial to Jarman's aesthetic use of history and religion. 'Obsessed by the interpretation of the past', as he confesses in the notes accompanying the *Caravaggio* script, Jarman frequently found filmic inspiration in the Elizabethan and Jacobean pasts. We have not only his cinematic version of Shakespeare's *The Tempest* (1979) and Marlowe's *Edward II* (1991); there is also the use of fourteen of Shakespeare's sonnets (read by the actress Judy Dench) on the sound-track of *The Angelic Conversation* (1985) and the presence of Elizabeth I, the astrologer-alchemist John Dee, and Ariel as a framing counterpoint to the scenes of contemporary British squalor and violence in *Jubilee* (1978). None of these films aims for 'historical accuracy'. *The Tempest* and *Edward II* have deliberately jarring reminders of late twentieth-century culture and politics: Elizabeth Welsh singing 'Stormy Weather' in the Shakespeare film, and, among other things, the shots of demonstrations by the gay and lesbian organization OutRage in *Edward II. Caravaggio* is also replete with anachronistic touches: the critic Baglione's typewriter, Ranuccio's motorbike, the gold calculator held by the financier Vincenzo Giustiniani. Jarman saw Caravaggio as a kind of legitimating model for such abrupt intrusions of contemporary life into predominantly period films. 'For Caravaggio the past was matter of fact – it lived in his own back yard.' He knew – as Jarman wished to know – 'how to present the present past'. 'Caravaggio was a turning point; a mere thirty years after him scientific method was on the ascendant and Poussin was deep in the archaeological portrayal of the antique.'[2]

More important than the anachronistic detail in making 'the present past' present is a willingness to grant a certain opacity to the materials being used to represent the past, an opacity that makes impossible the illusion of being able to read through those materials and see the past 'as it was'. In Caravaggio's case, this meant, as Jarman saw, '[burning] away decorum and the ideal, ... [knocking] the saints out of the sky and onto the streets'.[3] As we argue in *Caravaggio's Secrets*, there is a politically explosive potential in Caravaggio's implicit insistence that we recognize the present in the reconstruction of the past. Perhaps most forcefully in the late *St. John the Baptist* (1609–10; in the Galleria

Borghese, Rome), Caravaggio appears to be allowing his model to play his role unpersuasively, to insist that we recognize a Roman boy of the streets instead of St. John devoured by his ascetic passion. The opacity of the model's deteriorating flesh could be seen as the resistance of a contemporary body to a veritable industry of symbolization.[4] Compared with the insistence, on the part of Caravaggio's models, that we see *them* and not merely St. John or the dead Virgin, that we take account of their refusal to be *used for representation,* Jarman's jolting anachronisms (the typewriter in *Caravaggio*, the gay protest in *Edward II)* seem like rather crude attacks on an audience's willingness to go along with conventional realistic deceits. Jarman none the less saw in Caravaggio – and aimed for in his own work – what we take to be Caravaggio's rejection of both the claim that knowledge of the past (in art, its successful representation or re-creation) is either possible or useful, and the willingness to use this claim as a pretext for evading our responsibility to the present.

What Jarman principally recognized in Caravaggio, however, was his (presumed) homosexuality. Caravaggio 'brought the lofty ideals down to earth', Jarman wrote late in 1982 (during the fifth re-write of the script for his film), 'and became the most homosexual of painters, in the way that Pasolini is the most homosexual of film-makers'. Recognizing the difficulty of our knowing exactly 'how the seventeenth century understood physical homosexuality', Jarman none the less persisted – at least at this stage of his thought – in seeing Caravaggio as a gay hero in a homophobic culture. 'In a hostile environment [Caravaggio's] extremes of self-analysis ["he is the most self-conscious of artists"] became self-destruction.' When he wrote this, Jarman had not yet been diagnosed as HIV-positive, and his critique of Thatcherism in England had not yet become the angry, often powerful attacks on the homophobic insensitivity to those suffering and dying from AIDS which inform both his writing and the films (especially, *The Garden* [1990] and *Edward II)* of the late 80s and 90s. British homophobia, however, was obviously not invented for the AIDS epidemic, and, as the early texts on *Caravaggio* indicate, Jarman's attraction to the painter had much to do with his

perception of Caravaggio as a gay artist, like Pasolini and Jarman himself, having to struggle in a society hostile to 'the centre of his life'.[5]

Jarman's identification with Caravaggio as a homosexual did not always have such historical solemnity; it could also be more intimate, raunchier. Speaking of an avoidance of landscape common to Caravaggio's paintings and his own films, Jarman gives a sexy twist to this preference for interiors: 'We're both nocturnal back-room boys.' In a similar vein, he proposes an astonishing interpretation of Caravaggio's self-portrait in a figure to the far left in *The Martyrdom of St. Matthew (circa* 1599–1600*)*, a man apparently leaving the scene and looking over his shoulder at the young, massive, scantily clad executioner about to strike (or having just struck) with his sword the passive martyred saint lying beneath him:

The Martyrdom of St. Matthew, 1599–1600 by Michelangelo Merisi da Caravaggio (1571–1610), San Luigi dei Francesi, Rome, Italy/Bridgeman Art Library, London/New York

Michele [as Caravaggio is called in the film] gazes wistfully at the hero slaying the saint. It is a look no one can understand unless he has stood till 5 a.m. in a gay bar hoping to be fucked by that hero. The gaze of the passive homosexual at the object of his desire, he waits to be chosen, he cannot make the choice. Later his head will be cut off by a less godlike version of the young assassin; his name is now David and all the weight of society is behind him and he can cut off the head without a trace of pity.

The painting of *The Martyrdom of St. Matthew* plays an important role in Jarman's film. Caravaggio, erotically obsessed with Ranuccio Thomasoni, pays the young man to pose as the executioner; during one of the posing sessions there is a shot that imitates the corner of the painting just mentioned. (Elsewhere in the same volume, Jarman re-states his crude fantasy-reading of the painting: 'a handsome assassin … is cruised by the artist gazing guiltily over his shoulder.')[6] Michele's relation to Ranuccio is, however – as we shall see – far more complex, and interesting, than the passage just quoted suggests. Indeed, Jarman's film would not be worth talking about if he treated Caravaggio's homosexual desires at the level of his critical comments. We could of course also say that since the film is much better than the texts accompanying it would suggest, there's not much point in giving serious attention to the texts. There are, we feel, two good reasons for citing these passages. First, since the simplified relation

Michele in left corner of *The Martyrdom*

they assume between the victimized homosexual and an oppressive society is congenial to certain forms of queer politics, it has been picked up by Jarman's critics as a reason for praising his work. His films have in large measure been admired as acts of political resistance. In his introduction to a 1996 collection of essays devoted to Jarman's films, Chris Lippard speaks of Jarman 'as perhaps the most prominent queer man in Britain over the last decade'. Several of the contributors focus on Jarman as queer hero. Tracy Biga discusses the 'non-narrative organisation of Jarman's books and films', as well as 'their content and even their mode of production', as working 'continually against patriarchal hierarchy, as well as against other forms of hierarchy and authority'. In an essay entitled 'Perverse Law: Jarman as gay criminal hero', David Gardner reads Jarman's 'dark implication that homosexuality equals crime, love equals murder', not as complicating our sense of desire and identity in ways that might call for a re-thinking of contemporary queer politics, but rather as 'equations [that] open the way for struggle if they do not accede to the dominant notions of criminal and homosexual. In a resistant reading, they signal strength and activism: the shock value of a declaration of one's marginal desire, the insistence on one's existence, the dramatisation of the struggle itself.' In another contribution (with an equally confident title: 'Opposing "Heterosoc": Derek Jarman's counter-hegemonic activism'), Martin Quinn-Meyler also manages to see the violence frequently associated with homosexuality in Jarman's films not as compelling us to acknowledge certain complicities in homosexual desire with the very violence that oppresses us, but rather as 'always an act of subversion with the potential to destabilize the control of Heterosex'. 'Militarised queer sex' is always 'oppositional'; no matter how nasty it becomes, we can always count on 'militaristic and physically aggressive' queer lovemaking to come down on the side of the 'counter-hegemonic'. It is apparently only by maintaining this oppositional purity that Jarman could continue to be promoted – especially in the few years preceding his death from AIDS in 1994 – as, in Joseph A. Gomez's terms, 'Britain's most up-front and articulate advocate for homosexuality, and probably its most "in your face" critic of Thatcherite values – whether economic, political, social or aesthetic'.[7]

A few hours before the last page was written, we read an account of yet another hate crime in America. In Laramie, Wyoming, a state nearly as fabled for its right-wing politics as for its spectacular mountain views, a 21-year-old gay student was kidnapped by two young men, pistol-whipped and left unconscious tied to a ranch fence for eighteen hours until a passing bicyclist spotted him. He later died. (Wyoming is one of ten states that do not have hate-crime laws; such legislation has repeatedly been voted down on the grounds that it would give homosexuals special rights.) The girlfriend of one of the murderous straights, apparently in an effort to explain the violence, has reported that Matthew Shepard, the gay man, had made passes at one of his two attackers in a local bar, thereby 'embarrassing' him 'in front of all their friends'.[8] Probably the only morally healthy response to incidents like this one is a frankly and happily anti-liberal desire for capital punishment, or, at the very least, prolonged and public physical torture perhaps not unlike that inflicted on Shepard by these young heterosexuals so exceptionally sensitive to social-sexual 'embarrassment'. In the face of such horrific manifestations of homophobia, it may seem mean-spirited to claim, as we wish to do, that it is time to realize the inadequacy, for a queer politics and for a queer aesthetic, of anti-patriarchal stances and gay advocacy. It is normal enough to want to spit slogans of 'gay pride', 'compulsive heterosexuality', and 'queer superiority' in the faces of all those who would deny us not only the conjugal and family rights enjoyed by straight society, but even the more elemental right to live. And yet, even while being certain that homophobic violence (from name-calling to murder) is far from vanquished, we have perhaps had enough political victories, and we have surely become accustomed to a high enough level of reflection about our sexual identity, that we can afford to be somewhat critical of our by now-instinctive applause for 'gay is good' politics and art. Wouldn't it be possible both to act on our rightful rage at all the ways in which we continue to be denied full equality *and* to see how stultifying it is to praise someone for 'advocating' homosexuality (whatever that may mean)?

Jarman himself provided a rather messy answer to this question. Especially – and understandably – during the last few years of his life,

queer pride and queer anger come to be dominant themes in his work.
The published screenplay of *Edward II* is called *Queer Edward II*. The
book is 'dedicated to the repeal of all anti-gay laws', and, on the same
page as the dedication, Jarman announces that the play's 'only message'
is 'Marlowe outs the past – why don't we out the present?' to which he
adds what we are presumably meant to take as a tonic dismissal of all
that is irrelevant in literature: 'Fuck poetry.' The point is emphasized in
one of the notes that share each page of the book with the film's script:
'I chose this play solely for its subject. The poetry, like my production
values, is of secondary importance.'[9] The very shape of the book
emphasizes Jarman's choice: the film's script is on the left side of each
page, Jarman's comments on the production are on the right side, and, in
much larger letters at the top (and continued sometimes at the bottom)
of each page is a rallying queer slogan: 'Consenting Gay Sex is Not a
Crime,' 'Jesus Was a Drag Queen,' 'You Say Don't Fuck – We Say Fuck
You,' 'Don't Cry, Maybe You're Just Going Through a Straight Phase,'
'Heterosexuality Isn't Normal, it's Just Common,' 'I Wish *My* Father
Were a Lesbian' (apparently a reference to God, Jesus' father, who, in

Nigel Terry as Mortimer in *Edward II*

another defiant announcement is proclaimed to be a 'black Jewish lesbian'), 'Anus – the Last Place the Government Should Be Poking its Nose,' etc., etc. This, then, is 'Edward II/improved by Derek Jarman', as we read at the top of every two pages. It's all good queer fun, to be sure, but it is also evidence of Jarman's willingness to sell himself short for the sake of being immediately recognized and applauded by a particular audience. That willingness undoubtedly helped to make him famous, but it also had the unfortunate result of bringing him a fame that was a tribute to his limitations rather than to his very real talent.

Interestingly, Jarman's film *Edward II* is a much more problematic formulation of what may have been similar intentions. David Hawkes has succinctly summarized all the ways in which Jarman manipulates Marlowe's play in order to make the opposition between a heterosexist society and gay love its *only* subject. Jarman omits the passage in which the younger Mortimer explains his enmity toward Gaveston, Edward's lover, on the basis of the former's 'transgression of class boundaries, rather than

OutRage demonstration in *Edward II*

his sexual relations with the King'. The younger Mortimer's speech is in answer to his uncle's counsel that he let Edward 'without controlment have his will', for 'The mightiest Kings have had their minions.' 'And [Mortimer, senior] goes on, as Jarman puts it, to "open the classical closet", listing the homosexual affairs of heroes and philosophers.' Significantly, Jarman gives this speech to the more sympathetic Kent, Edward's brother, and Mortimer is presented as 'overtly homophobic – as he beats Spencer, he calls him "girl boy" (a line not found in Marlowe, but apparently coined by the actor, Nigel Terry)'. The film sets up highly tendentious oppositions between gay desire and straight desire, between gay fun and straight fun. Thus, 'we are shown Edward and Gaveston being entertained by male strippers, boys in the gym, and a naked rugby scrum; Mortimer fulminates about Edward's salacious reputation while himself deeply engrossed in a heterosexual S&M scene.'[10] The effects of these transformations are complex. For one thing, we are given a psychological cliché: Mortimer is power-hungry, *therefore* (Jarman's argument implicitly goes) he gets his kicks from being overpowered. More interestingly, the yoking together of homophobia and resentment of the high titles bestowed by Edward on 'one so basely born' as Gaveston[11] suggests that the real danger in homosexuality – perhaps obscurely sensed by Edward's enemies – is an inherent indifference to those hierarchical distinctions that not only reinforce power relations but also serve to make social life intelligible. *Edward II* doesn't go much farther than a partial redistributing of those distinctions, but it also strips them of any political significance. For all the claustrophobic atmosphere of Jarman's indoor castle set (the people are totally shut out of this power struggle), his gay lovers are curiously 'outside' the castle. With their improvised, and marginalized, entertainments, they merely pass time – as if they were suspended between a community of established titles and functions and a sociality not yet defined, but perhaps initiated by a kind of democratic sexuality. As Jarman saw, this doesn't necessarily make his gay heroes always likeable. If Edward is for the most part presented sympathetically, Jarman allowed Andrew Tiernan to play Gaveston 'in a way that will [not] endear me to "Gay Times"'.[12] Politically correct or not, Gaveston's repulsiveness is crucial to the film's refusal to 'justify' its uncompromising defence of Edward's right to desire – a justification that might have made the object of his desire appealing to those who would claim to judge if the king's lover is 'worthy' of that right.

Finally, however, in the case of Isabella, what Hawkes calls her 'hyper-heterosexuality', while intended to sharpen the opposition between good gays and bad straights, actually blurs the opposition. Jarman so exaggerates her transformation (present in Marlowe) from Edward's loyal and unhappily loving wife to a cruel enemy obsessed with stealing his power that she may begin to elicit our sympathy – not exactly as an independent character but rather as a fantasy-projection still clinging, as it were, to her creator. Jarman gives her some nasty lines Marlowe gave to the barons, and with vampiric relish she murders Kent with a sensuous bite on the neck. As we will see in *Caravaggio*, the 'misogynous' label, which has been applied to Jarman, is seriously inadequate to his representation of women. This is also true for *Edward II*, but not because, as in the case of *Caravaggio*, a woman provides the *only* desired intimacy, but rather because misogyny is too 'rationalized' and too conscious a category to describe anything like the grotesque horror of Isabella's representation. It is perhaps because Jarman thought himself willing to 'fuck poetry', and may even have believed that he was only interested in the 'subject' of *Edward II* (the oppression of queer desire by heterosexist society) that 'poetry' – more precisely in this case, film – could, as it were, so easily take its revenge on him. His film exceeds his thematic intention in part by being more radical than that intention (by proposing homosexuality's aptitude for setting itself free of given modes of relationality), but also by exposing the ease with which, for example, supposedly political statements about heterosexist lust for power can be exposed as a hateful fantasy about women. The refusal to think with any complexity about the presumed opposition between queer virtue and straight vice leads to a different sort of complexity (we will see other examples of this): that of a troubled psyche.

The slogans of the *Queer Edward II* text smother such ambiguities before they can even arise. The queer political theme reigns

unchallenged. The OutRage protest demonstration is a rally *within*
Jarman's film; *Queer Edward II is* a gay and lesbian rally. Jarman happily
fails at times – most notably, in *Caravaggio* – to reduce his work to the
status of a rally, although we will also see that he perversely spends
considerable energy trying to hide that failure. The rally mentality has
been a largely unfortunate by-product of the increased visibility of gays
and lesbians in recent years. In the interests of the community solidarity
necessary for effective political action, that mentality is obviously
desirable. (In Jarman's work, the journalistic militancy of the late
autobiography, *At Your Own Risk / A Saint's Testament* [1993], is
wonderfully effective.) But it has also become a part of our intellectual
life. It often seems, for example, that there is a new standard of
excellence in academic conferences: audiences warmly receive what they
already know and agree with. There is nothing surprising, or harmful,
about this in political rallies, but it doesn't do much for original thinking.
Intellectual investigations easily become occasions for self-recognition
and self-congratulation, occasions that leave little room for the frictions
that nourish thought. Our audiences tend to be those who already agree
with what we have to say – which doesn't leave much room, or tolerance,
for questioning the value of the rights we are unjustly deprived of (such
as marriage). While fighting for those rights, gays and lesbians might also
be thinking, as it were, to the side of them – in a 'place' that questions
the very assumptions about relationality that have led in the first place to
the privileging of conjugal intimacy as a superior form of relationship.

Jarman *could* be refreshingly perverse about queer identity, even in
his written work. A passage in still another autobiographical text, *Kicking
the Pricks*, gives an amusing and original twist to discussions of the
aetiology of homosexual desire. Speaking of his father's determination to
impose his own austerity on his family, Jarman writes: 'It's the classic
fag's father. Thank God they exist, and thank God I had one. After all,
childhood only lasts to puberty, then one has the rest of one's life to
enjoy oneself unravelling the damage. It's the most distressing sight to
see happy families, nothing good can come to them.'[13] The passage ends
on a note of queer smugness, but, in its substance, it is, as we like to say,

more 'gay-friendly' than the knee-jerk queer rejection of the familiar psychoanalytic account of homosexuality it defiantly embraces. It suggests – very lightly, to be sure – that even the explanation most frequently associated with homophobic reductionism in the history of psychoanalysis might be turned to gay advantage. The 'unhealthy' lack of supportive affection from the father – unhealthy from the perspective of a normative development toward genital heterosexuality – might in fact be crucial in nourishing that aversion to patriarchal authority in the name of which many queer thinkers recoil in horror from such ill-intentioned psychoanalytic clichés. To put it crudely, the gay way of getting fucked up by family ties (or the lack of them) may be more valuable, more civilizing, than the straight way.

More interesting than this, however (we have, after all, been looking at a passing remark in Jarman's autobiographical writing), is Jarman's total indifference, in the film *Caravaggio,* to the oppositional politics he seemed so ready to embrace. Unlike *Edward II* and *The Garden, Caravaggio* neither victimizes nor exalts gay love. You would never guess from the film that during a long period in its preparation Jarman seriously thought he was making a film about 'the most homosexual of painters', one who 'took on the Church as his true and deadly enemy' since it had outlawed 'the centre of his life'.[14] Probably more faithful to early seventeenth-century sexual politics than the comparison of Caravaggio's fate to Pasolini's, Jarman's film represents a notable indifference to sexual orientation. Libertinage is the ecclesiastical rule of the day – whether it be the mild, extremely refined homo-eroticism of Caravaggio's patron, Cardinal Del Monte, the kinky heterosexuality of Cardinal Scipione Borghese (who, removing Lena's slipper and kissing her foot at the party in the Catacombs, calls the girl of the Roman streets 'Madonna! Queen of Heaven!'), or the raunchy suggestiveness of Pope Paul V (who, during the interview with Caravaggio who has been commissioned to paint his portrait, addresses him as 'you little bugger'). It's not simply that *Caravaggio* fails to represent homosexual desire as 'counter-hegemonic'; the whole question of its hegemonic status is implicitly dismissed as irrelevant to the film's profound treatment of

various registers of desire. Finally, however, the exceptionally rich cinematic reflection on art, violence and desire in *Caravaggio* is the product of the same sensibility responsible for the visually glamorized pieties about gay love in *The Garden* and the queer rallying spirit of

Top: Michael Gough as Cardinal del Monte. Bottom: Lena meets Cardinal Scipione Borghese

Edward II – and this, we feel, helps to explain the limitations of even Jarman's most impressive work. It will be especially instructive to look at those limitations in the context of Jarman's loving meditation on the work and art of another artist who didn't suffer from them. It was – to return to the question with which we opened our discussion – what Jarman *didn't* learn from Caravaggio that will allow us to speculate about the bases for what we can't help but recognize as different orders of greatness in art.

II

Caravaggio was made in an old London docklands warehouse for £475,000 from the British Film Institute. Shooting began in August 1985 and lasted six weeks. The 93-minute film was Jarman's fifth full-length feature, and the first to be filmed directly in 35mm. (During the 1970s, he had made several short films in Super-8, and his other longer films were originally shot in 8mm or 16mm, and then blown up to 35mm.) Jarman had been working on the Caravaggio project for several years:

In May 1978 I took a train to Rome after my film *Jubilee* opened at the Cannes Film Festival. I booked myself into a small hotel near the Spanish Steps and wrote the first of the scripts for a film on the painter Michele Caravaggio. I certainly didn't imagine then that this film was going to occupy the next seven years of my life; fortunately I'm not clairvoyant, as I'm sure that if I had known there were to be seventeen more scripts and a dozen more trips to Rome pursuing this elusive project, I'd have dumped the carefully bound results in the attic along with another half dozen or so scripts labelled 'maybe'. But each time I was about to knife Caravaggio, the words 'No hope no fear' – engraved on the painter's dagger – would flash into mind, I would catch the glint of gold and begin the process of refinement once again.[15]

The opening chapter of the 1984 autobiography *Dancing Ledge* describes various moments in what came to seem like an endless process of revision and re-writing. From the very beginning, Jarman was certain about where the material for his life of Caravaggio would come from.

'When I left Rome in July [1978] I had completed the first script which
was based on a reading of the paintings rather than the biographies of
Baglione or Mancini.' Jarman admired Caravaggio, as we have seen, for
his indifference to the 'scientific method' that would lead Poussin to
'the archeological portrayal of the antique'. Knocking the saints out of
the sky, Caravaggio made street-life of seventeenth-century Rome visible
in his paintings. For Jarman, being faithful to this aspect of Caravaggio
meant different things. His least interesting temptation during the long
gestation period was to include references to his own life within the film
and, at the extreme, to re-cast the entire biography in a contemporary
setting. 'In this rewrite,' he noted in 1981, 'I'm going to filter in my own
life. My Italian childhood in Villa Quessa would make a perfect start, a
few miles down the road from Caravaggio.' But in the fourth re-write, a
year later, Jarman was 'writing himself out': his presence in the film as
protagonist and onlooker had 'brought the piece to life' but 'left a
certain confusion'. He would also write the present out of the film,
although in 1982 Jarman was still inclined to feel that while the film
should be faithful to 'the structures of ideology and power' of the
beginning of the seventeenth century, 'only by making Caravaggio a
contemporary will we see how revolutionary a painter he was'. Jarman
gives us a not-too-promising hint of how this mixture of past and
present would have been managed when he writes that if the power
structures were to be those of Caravaggio's time, the street-girl Lena
would have to be 'a sort of romantic gypsy dancer' rather than a
seventeenth-century whore, and we would see her 'sitting by the side of
the Via Appia in a white fur coat'. In any case, a few months later, in
January 1983, Jarman records 'a sudden decision to rewrite the film in
period or an approximation of period'. Modernization would risk
becoming 'the *cause célèbre* of the film at the expense of content and
would destroy its subtler shades. In period, perhaps a gentler, less brash
effect and greater depth would result.'[16] Indeed, without giving in to the
showy, self-conscious historicism of the period films he detested, Jarman
– except for the few anachronistic touches mentioned earlier – quite
comfortably and quite persuasively situates Caravaggio in his own time

and place, implicitly dismissing factitious concerns for both historical authenticity and modern relevance.

Jarman's biography of Caravaggio is his interpretation of Caravaggio's painting. The film finally made in 1985 is, as Jarman said of his first script (written in 1978), largely 'based on a reading of the paintings'.[17] This is not to say that the correspondences have a programmatic consistency. There is, most notably, no pictorial inspiration for the character of Jerusaleme, Caravaggio's mute helper, although he does come to embody one of Jarman's two divergent readings of the St. John the Baptist paintings. On the one hand, these paintings inspire Jarman's portrait of Ranuccio Thomasoni, the man Caravaggio murdered in 1606. Our only historical source of this violent incident in Caravaggio's life is a Notice dated 31 May of that year according to which, as a result of a fight in the Campo Marzo over a bet of ten *scudi* on a tennis match, Caravaggio fatally wounded a certain Ranuccio of Terni. Jarman notes that when Caravaggio died in Porto Ercole four years after fleeing Rome following the murder of Ranuccio, he left with his belongings a painting of St. John the Baptist which Jarman identifies as the one now in Kansas City. The painting was done in Rome a couple of years before the Campo

Ranuccio poses as St. John the Baptist

Marzo incident; Caravaggio carried it with him during all the years of exile. In the annotated *Caravaggio* script Jarman asks: 'Why was the painting of a naked youth so important for the artist?' He finds 'a clue to this mystery' in the Malta *Beheading of St. John the Baptist* (1608), Caravaggio's only signed painting, in which the signature is scrawled into the saint's blood on the floor, and reads 'I, Caravaggio, did this.' Jarman interprets 'I did this' as Caravaggio's confession of the murder of his lover – the model for the other St. John painting to which he was apparently so attached. In the note from the *Caravaggio* script, Jarman associates the drama he has read into the St. John paintings with the melancholy desire he sees in Caravaggio's self-portrait in *The Martyrdom of St. Matthew*. Caravaggio paints himself 'cruising' the executioner, 'staring wistfully over his shoulder at a beautiful naked youth. A murderer, who he has painted triumphantly.' So the murdered lover may have been originally a desired murderer. Jarman even suggests that the murderer's real victim in the early St. Matthew painting is not the saint but rather the painter to whom the executioner's back is turned. Jarman connects *The Martyrdom of St. Matthew* with the late *David With the Head of Goliath* (1609–10), in which the painter's role as victim is no longer displaced: Caravaggio painted his own features on Goliath's severed head. By the end of the paragraph in which this connection is made, Jarman is reading both paintings as showing 'martyrdom at the hands of youth'.[18] As we saw earlier, Jarman felt that no one could understand the painter's wistful gaze at 'the hero slaying the saint' in *The Martyrdom of St. Matthew* 'unless he has stood until 5 a.m. in a gay bar hoping to be fucked by that hero'. By now we have the outlines of a novel of unhappy gay desire: 'martyred' by the murderously indifferent Ranuccio, Caravaggio may kill him in an act of desperately unhappy love. After the murder, he will carry with him for four years the portrait of his dead lover, and in one of his last paintings he will confess to the deed.

This is indeed a biography 'based on a reading of the paintings'. More exactly, it is a biography in which a single attested biographical fact – Caravaggio's murder of Ranuccio Thomasoni – is novelized by way of a highly selective, highly personal reading and juxtaposition of a few paintings. The process is not without interest as the basis of a filmic biography, but the most interesting fact about it is how little it corresponds to Jarman's film. Michele does indeed kill Ranuccio, but for the love of whom? He slashes the young man's throat in response to the latter's confession that he murdered his lover Lena. 'I did it for you', Ranuccio cries, 'for love!' Here is the rest of this sequence:

> MICHELE: For what?
> RANUCCIO: For love!
> *The light goes out on* MICHELE's *face. He looks astounded. It has never crossed his mind that* RANUCCIO *might be the murderer.*
> MICHELE: You murdered her? You murdered her!
> RANUCCIO: For you. *He smiles.* For us!
> MICHELE *pulls his knife. He stares at* RANUCCIO *for what seems an eternity. Then suddenly he strikes, cutting* RANUCCIO's *throat. The blood spurts everywhere.* RANUCCIO's *hand tries to staunch it. He covers* MICHELE's *face with the blood in a mirror-image of the earlier knife fight. Then he throws his arms around him in a vice-like grip. Slowly the grip relaxes and he sinks to the ground, dead.*[19]

Michele's murder of Ranuccio ends up being filmed as something quite different from a *crime passionnel*. Or if it is a crime of passion, it's not at all certain that Ranuccio is the object of that passion. (By no means incidentally, there is no indication in the film that Michele and Ranuccio ever become physical lovers, or, if they don't, that Michele suffers from this.) In the discussion of the making of *Caravaggio* in *Dancing Ledge*, Jarman writes: '[Caravaggio] paints his lovers as St. John, the wild one in the wilderness, who will be destroyed by a capricious woman.'[20] If Jarman takes inspiration from the story of St. John the Baptist and Salome in imagining the fate of Caravaggio's model for St. John, it is in order to radically shift the terms of that story. In abandoning Ranuccio for the rich Cardinal Scipione Borghese, Lena could perhaps be thought of as 'destroying' him 'capriciously'. But it is he who kills her, and if we were to stick to the presumed sources for their portrayal in Jarman's film, we would have to say that Jarman has St. John murder Salome. But Lena is by no means a Salome-like figure, and if she poses as Mary Magdalen early in her pregnancy, Caravaggio also uses her dead body as his model for *Death of the Virgin* (1605–6).

Top: Ranuccio confesses to Lena's murder. Bottom: Michele avenges Lena.
Opposite: Lena as Caravaggio's Mary Magdalen

At the beginning of this discussion of Ranuccio, we mentioned two quite different readings of the St. John the Baptist paintings. Jarman finds in them not only clues to Caravaggio's love for his model (or models: Jarman writes that 'he paints his *lovers* as St. John'), but also an indication of Caravaggio seeing himself as Christ. It is this reading of the paintings – and not the inference of a violent sexual drama – that figures prominently in the film. When Michele returns to his studio after the party in the Catacombs, he finds Jerusaleme posing – apparently for himself – as St. John. He duplicates – or replaces? – Ranuccio posing as the Saint in an earlier scene. Jerusaleme is decidedly not one of Caravaggio's lovers, but in the film it is he – and no one else – whom Michele explicitly identifies as St. John. 'You are my St. John,' he says to his helper, 'and this,' he adds, surveying his studio, 'is our wilderness.' So the one who prepares Caravaggio's paint is the one who prepares the world for Caravaggio–Christ – as if Jarman had read into the St. John the Baptist paintings not the key to an unhappy, violent homosexual affair, but rather the inspiration for an entirely invented character who would prepare the painter's materials. Jerusaleme is also Michele's most constant companion: only he is with the painter at Porto Ercole when his beloved master dies.

If the relation between St. John and Jesus is thereby transformed into a relation of *work* between the painter and his helper, the fate of the Messiah announced by John the Baptist enters the work in a nearly literal fashion. In the extraordinary *tableau vivant* of Caravaggio's *Entombment* (1602–4) at the end of the film, the dead Christ's head is Caravaggio's head. This is Jarman's invention: the dead Christ is not one of the historical Caravaggio's self-portraits. By this time, Jarman's film has given to Caravaggio's life the extraordinary religious significance Jarman found in his paintings. He spoke of him as 'a man who understands the Passion, the most powerful religious painter of the Renaissance'. It is as if Jarman read Caravaggio's paintings as demanding so imperiously that the painter's life resonate with the Christian meanings of the work that Jarman can actually 'correct' *The Entombment* (and it is entirely Jarman's correction: Michele is not painting that *tableau vivant*) so that it may represent its power in the painter's life. In *Dancing Ledge*, Jarman writes that Caravaggio's self-portraits don't merely 'represent, but anticipate and instigate the life itself'.[21] Almost four hundred years before Jarman's film, Caravaggio would already have been basing his life on a reading of his paintings. Jarman takes the process one step further: in *his Entombment* the life instigated by the painting inspires the painting itself. Caravaggio's identification with his painting's subject retrospectively *becomes* the subject of the painting.

Lena the dead Virgin, Caravaggio the dead Christ: the closeness between Michele and Lena, which begins the day the painter gives her a dress and jewels to wear in the Catacombs the night his *Profane Love* (1601–2) is unveiled, is, toward the end of Jarman's film, elevated, in astonishing fashion, to the relation between Christ and his virgin mother. We will have more to say about that relation; for the moment, we mention it as our final example of Jarman's extrapolating a life of Caravaggio from his own responses to the paintings. From our present perspective, what is most striking about this particular reading is how different it is from Jarman's emphasis, in his writing, on the identification of Ranuccio Thomasoni as Caravaggio's cruel lover, and on the drama of

Jerusaleme poses as St. John the Baptist

Caravaggio's unhappy love for him. Something else was happening, something Jarman doesn't mention. He was looking intently not only at all those celebrated scenes of decapitation (and reading them as both a confession of the murder of the beloved Ranuccio–St. John and, especially in the David and Goliath painting, as a self-inflicted punishment for that crime), but also at two illustrious deaths that inaugurated Christianity: Christ's death on the Cross and that of the Virgin Mary. But this looking is nowhere reported – except in the film to which it eventually gave rise. It is not a secret reading – it is displayed in the film for everyone to see – but it is apparently one that can't be said. This is especially striking given Jarman's volubility about his films. There is a text for nearly every one of the feature films: *Kicking the Pricks* to accompany *The Last of England* and *The Angelic Conversation*, the heavily annotated scripts of *Edward II* and *Caravaggio* (in addition to the chapter in *Dancing Ledge* on the long history of preparing the latter film), the sections on *Jubilee* and *The Tempest* in *Dancing Ledge* and the reflection on colours, *Chroma*, at the time of Jarman's monochromatic final film, *Blue* (1993). But there is only silence surrounding the strangest, most powerful element of Jarman's most powerful film. *It can be shown, but it can't be said.* Jarman's work, for all its silence about this, is an extraordinary psychic unveiling. *Caravaggio*, however, goes so far as to propose the inadequacy of such self-exposures. Profoundly faithful in this respect to Caravaggio himself, it even begins – and we will have to recognize that it only begins – to expose its own structure of anxious desire as bringing us only to the threshold of the aesthetic. The disclosure of Being which perhaps only art brings about necessitates a leaving behind – a forgetting – of individual desires and individual identities.

III

'This film,' Jarman writes at the end of the *Caravaggio* script, 'is the first in which I have developed acting parts and bowed to narrative: a necessity imposed by the situation and a reflection of Caravaggio's style.'[22] In effect, Jarman uses in *Caravaggio* a conventional narrative structure unusual in his work. Very different in this respect from the apparently directionless succession (and explosion) of images in *The Last of England* (1987) and *The Garden*, *Caravaggio* gives us a straightforward chronological narrative of the years Caravaggio spent in Rome. There is nothing of the painter's life before his arrival in Rome, and nothing from the four years of exile in Naples, Malta and Sicily. Within the Roman period, the film moves, in conventional biographical fashion, from Michele at twenty selling art on the streets of Rome to the murder of Ranuccio Thomasoni in 1606 (after which the historical Caravaggio had to flee Rome). Even within this brief period, Jarman is highly selective, although in ways that don't disrupt the film's narrative intelligibility. After the early scenes of Michele hustling his paintings (and his body) and meeting the Cardinal del Monte (in whose palace he will live and work for the next few years), Jarman focuses almost entirely on the painter's involvement with Ranuccio and Lena. This selective biography is presented as a flashback; it is both framed and interrupted several times by scenes in the monastic hospital room at Porto Ercole where the painter is dying. Again, a conventional narrative device from realistic cinema, one for which Jarman seems to have had a special affection. He

The hospital room at Porto Ercole

used it at different moments in his career, both in films that 'bow to narrative' (*Caravaggio* and *Edward II*, the main body of which is a flashback as the jailed king remembers the events that have led to his imprisonment), and in the less conventionally structured *Jubilee*, where the sequences with Elizabeth I, John Dee and Ariel contain (at once frame and partially discipline) the scenes of random violence – and punk domestic life – from the reign of the contemporary Elizabeth. (Amusingly, it is Wittgenstein the boy who 'remembers' the life of Wittgenstein the man in Jarman's filmic biography of the philosopher [1992].)

The voice-overs that accompany the scenes of Caravaggio on his death-bed are the painter's recollections of both his life in Rome and, from his boyhood, his passionate friendship with Pasqualone. (The latter appears only once in the film, in a scene that, for reasons we will be discussing, can hardly be called a flashback. In Caravaggio's life, a notary named Pasqualone accused the painter of attacking him after having 'had words' with Caravaggio 'on account of a woman called Lena, who is to be found on her feet in the Piazza Navona [a location for prostitutes] … who is Caravaggio's woman'.[23] As a childhood friend of the painter,

Michele buys Jerusaleme, his helper

Pasqualone is Jarman's invention, and seems to be a transposition of a young Italian named Davide with whom Jarman as a boy became infatuated during the brief period he and his parents lived near Lake Maggiore. Jarman would later refer to 'this innocent idyll' as 'my great secret'.[24] His equivalent in the film does not have a name; there is, however, a Davide: a waiter in the Bar del Moro and Michele's occasional model and lover.) The only chronological violation once the flashbacks start is in the first one. Michele's voice-over the first time we see him on his hospital death-bed ends with an address to his faithful Jerusaleme, who, sobbing, is attending him: 'To think, Jerusaleme, our friendship should end in this room – this cold white room so far from home.' We switch immediately after this to a very differently lighted room, one plunged in a partially illuminated darkness reminiscent of the chiaroscuro of Caravaggio's work. It was in this shepherd's hut in the Abruzzi hills many years earlier that Michele had bought Jerusaleme, who, unable to speak, would have been, as a voice-over in the script that's not used in the film tells us, 'no use as a shepherd – a burden to his poor family'.[25] After this and the next scene, in which the painter brings the boy to his studio in Rome, we move to an earlier period and the flashbacks proceed in chronological order. (The actor who will play the mature Caravaggio – Nigel Terry – appears in the two early Jerusaleme scenes, but for the next few evocations of the painter's past, until his installation in Del Monte's palace, the younger Caravaggio is played by Dexter Fletcher.)

Michele first sees Ranuccio (played by Sean Bean) gambling with other workmen in the Bar del Moro. The painter is interested, but Davide warns him: 'You won't get anywhere with him,' and asks: 'Why don't you paint him?' Caravaggio is working, with great difficulty, on the first version of the painting that will make him famous – *The Martyrdom of St. Matthew* – which he describes to Davide as 'the most successful disaster in Rome'. Soon after, immediately following a New Year's Eve celebration at the painter's studio – it is the year 1600 – Michele sees Ranuccio again, this time at a prize fight at the fair. A fascinated Caravaggio watches the young man brutally beat Davide to the ground.

Nigel Terry as Caravaggio

Dexter Fletcher as the young
Caravaggio

Ranuccio's girl Lena kisses him; Michele joins them and hands Ranuccio a golden coin. The motif of golden coins is picked up spectacularly in the next scene, where we see Ranuccio posing for the definitive version of *The Martyrdom*. As he paints, Michele throws coins to Ranuccio, who sticks them into his mouth until, Jarman writes in the script, 'it was

Top: Ranuccio and Davide fight. Bottom: Ranuccio's 'golden scream'

contorted into a golden scream',[26] and, we might add, it comes to resemble the executioner's open mouth in Caravaggio's painting. At the end of this scene, Michele, with a coin half-protruding from his mouth, approaches Ranuccio, who bites the coin into his own mouth from between the painter's lips. The gold coins serve as an erotic toy in the following scene: Lena and Ranuccio caress each other with them, and, as she kisses him, she tries to extract a coin he has hidden in his mouth. The next stage of the Michele–Ranuccio relation is a knife-fight between the two in the painter's studio. When the painter relaxes his guard, thinking the fight is over, a treacherous Ranuccio stabs him in the side. Michele, taking some blood from his wound, wipes it on the young man's face, saying 'Blood brothers'. Ranuccio laughs, and kisses Caravaggio on the lips. Their relation is, then, initiated, punctuated, and ended by acts of physical violence. They meet at Ranuccio's fight with Davide; their one erotic contact consists of Ranuccio 'returning' Michele's blood to him from his own blood-smeared face; and when the painter slits Ranuccio's throat, the latter will repeat Michele's gesture from the earlier scene, smearing his blood on Michele's face just before dying in his arms.

Ranuccio stabs Michele

The momentous shift in their intimacy, which leads to this final act of violence, begins with the preparations for the party in the Catacombs which the immensely rich Vincenzo Giustiniani gives for the unveiling of *Profane Love* (*Amor vincit omnia*), commissioned by him from Caravaggio. Lena's costume for the party arrives on a day when Ranuccio is posing for that presumably revealing *St. John the Baptist* (carried by the painter during his years of exile from Rome, and in which Jarman read Caravaggio's passion for the man he murdered). In an astonishing reversal of the role Jarman gives to that painting in his writing, he films Ranuccio posing for it as the occasion of Caravaggio's turning away from him. In a striking shot, Jarman has Michele pin a pair of earrings to Lena's ears with Ranuccio between them in the background, still in his pose for the painting, looking lost and surly and giving a wholly unexpected sense to the young saint's dejected look in that Caravaggio work. The killing of Ranuccio has begun.

Some comic relief in the Catacombs is provided by Caravaggio's fierce critic Giovanni Baglione, whom we also see in his bathtub typing a vituperative attack on the painter. (The typewriter isn't the only

Ranuccio jealously watches Michele and Lena

anachronistic touch: the scene also refers, two centuries ahead of time, to David's painting *The Death of Marat*.) Unable to find an actor's agent willing to come up with a twelve-year-old boy who would be the naked model for Caravaggio's Cupid, Jarman cast the actress Dawn Archibald in the role as Pipo, a male model who poses fully clothed for the painting and unveils it as Giustiniani's party. It is here that Lena meets the man for whom she will soon leave Ranuccio: Cardinal Scipione Borghese, the rich and powerful nephew of the Pope. While posing as Mary Magdalen for Michele, Lena reveals to him that she is pregnant, a piece of news the painter communicates to an infuriated Ranuccio. Accompanied by two heavy bodyguards, a transformed Lena, now 'poised, elegant and collected' (she is played by the brilliant Tilda Swinton, featured in several

Top: Baglione after typing his attack against Michele. Bottom: Pipo as Cupid

of Jarman's films), makes a brief visit to the slum house. When Ranuccio asks: 'The child? Whose?' she answers only 'Mine' ('Mine and mine alone' in the script), and to her former lover's pathetic question 'What about us?' she brutally answers 'You have Michele. I have Scipione. And the child shall be rich beyond avarice.' But in the next scene we see Lena's dead body floating in the river, a scene for which Jarman's crew went to the riverbank, rigged up the lights and waited until 'the sun came out and turned the Thames into a sea of gold'.[27] Lena's muddy corpse is laid on a table in Caravaggio's studio; we see Michele combing her hair and Jerusaleme washing her feet. Ranuccio, seemingly despairing and protesting his innocence (he cries out that Scipione killed her), is imprisoned.

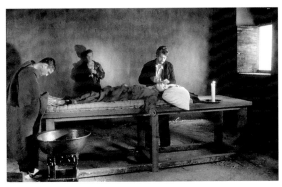

Top: Lena's corpse floats on the river. Bottom: Michele, Jerusaleme and Ranuccio attend Lena's dead body

In Caravaggio's studio, the transfiguration of Lena is under way. Lena's body and the mourners surrounding her bier become the models for Caravaggio's great altarpiece, *Death of the Virgin.* Michele moves between painting Lena and cradling her body in his arms. At the end of this powerful scene with the dead Virgin in his studio, Caravaggio turns angrily toward the camera, toward us, crying out: 'God curse you! You!' as if we had committed a blasphemy in seeing what we have just seen. (In the hospital at Porto Ercole, Caravaggio, violently fighting off a priest's attempt to put a crucifix in his hands, is about to die.) During Michele's meeting with Paul V the day he begins his portrait, the Pope agrees to release Ranuccio 'if the portrait looks good', and also as a favour to a painter whose paintings of the poor in religious altarpieces are judged by the church to be 'potent weapons against Satan and the Protestants'.[28] Ranuccio is freed and, in the scene mentioned earlier, returns, excited and smiling, to Michele, whom he congratulates on having 'pulled it off. Fucking brilliant. We've tricked the bastards.' It turns out to be Michele that Ranuccio has 'tricked', at least until now, leading him to think that Scipione was responsible for Lena's death. Michele pulls out his knife and cuts Ranuccio's throat.

In the film's final voice-over, Michele again invokes his childhood love: 'I bury my head in the pillow and dream of my true love, Pasqualone. I am rowing to you on the great dark ocean.' This is immediately followed by *Caravaggio*'s strongest, and most haunting, sequence. The script identifies an Easter procession of many years before in a square of the village of Caravaggio. The child Michele, dressed as an angel, and Pasqualone watch a procession of penitents passing by. But it is hard to believe that this Michele could become, in ten years or so, the rough boy-painter of the streets we saw at the beginning of the film. The voice and appearance are more refined; the boy appears to belong to a more prosperous social class than the young man he will presumably become – the comfortable middle class, say, of Jarman's upbringing. The irrelevance of realistic criteria of time and of identity is emphasized by what happens next. The boy opens some curtains to the side of the procession, walks through the doorway, and calls to Pasqualone to join

Top: Lena becomes the dead Virgin. Middle: Michele cradles the dead Lena.
Bottom: Michele curses us

Jack Birkett as Pope Paul V.

Easter procession of penitents

Deposition (*Entombment*), 1602–4 by Michelangelo Merisi da Caravaggio (1571–1610),
Vatican Museums and Galleries, Vatican City, Italy/Bridgeman Art Library, London/New York

Jarman-Caravaggio's *Entombment* scene.

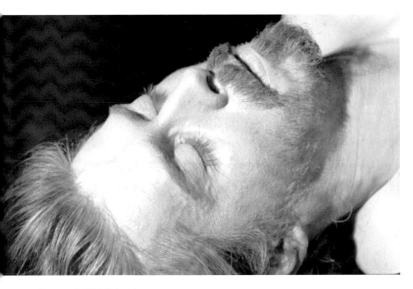

Caravaggio-Christ's head

him. They have entered a place – but where is this place? – in which Caravaggio's *Entombment of Christ* has come to life. Unlike the earlier *tableaux vivants* of Caravaggio's paintings, this one is not realistically accounted for as a pose from which the painter is working. Indeed the painter is dead; when we have a close-up of Christ's head, it is the dead Michele's head. Jarman represents, we suggested earlier, the power of art to 'instigate' the artist's life; but he has imagined the instigation – in this case, the painter's identification with his crucified subject – as an *effect* on the painting itself, as if the work had been 'postponed' until its power over its creator could be shown within it. Shown, of course, by Jarman, who, with this revision of the *Entombment*, signals to us his own implication in his film, the impossibility of his standing outside, of maintaining that perhaps always implausible distance between the creator and his creation.

It's not necessary for Jarman to be in his film as a recognizable presence (as he is, for example, in *The Last of England* and *The Garden*). Rather, he enters his work through a loving betrayal of its subject. The *Entombment* scene is not the first time we notice discrepancies between Caravaggio's paintings and the way they are (re-)painted in the models' poses and on the canvases of Jarman's Michele. The film is clearly not trying to get the paintings 'right'. In the *Entombment* scene, for example, Christ's body is tilted more toward the viewer than in Caravaggio's painting, with the result that we see more of Christ's loin-cloth and legs; the Virgin's arms are more open and her head is raised; all this in addition to the substitution of Michele's head for Christ's. If by that substitution Jarman wishes to propose Caravaggio's identification with Christ, he also suggests his own identification with Caravaggio by practically re-doing his work. He is so powerfully attached to the painter that he can't help being somewhat unfaithful to him. Thus *Caravaggio*'s flashbacks both begin and end with temporal infractions. The first merely violates chronology: the taking on of Jerusaleme took place after the scenes that immediately follow it. With the Easter procession sequence, it is a question not of a temporal displacement of episodes but rather of the erasure of narrative time itself. The sequence 'takes place' in

Michele's childhood; but it's not at all certain that the boy is Michele, and, if he is, it would be difficult to locate the 'time' when he might have come upon a scene from one of his own works painted twenty-five years later. But we are of course not *in* time. More exactly, the sequence can't help but take time (our time), but there is no time it represents. It is a figural metaphor deployed in cinematic time, a metaphor for the multiplication of the artist's identity in the working time of his art. The film's final scene brings us back to Porto Ercole, and to the dead Michele surrounded by a group of mourners. The connections between the two scenes are striking: there is the same religious music in both; Michele, like Christ, is attended by three women (two of them are the peasant women referred to in the script and whom we have seen in an earlier sequence standing at the hospital room door and who are now at the painter's bedside); the two men in Michele's room were in the *Entombment tableau vivant*. Three identities are displaced and condensed in these two scenes of death: Christ's, Caravaggio's, Jarman's.

Finally, the identification of Jarman with Caravaggio, and of Caravaggio with Christ, naturally infuses Caravaggio's death (and

The dead Michele and his mourners

Jarman's) with the sense of a martyrdom, of a death at the hands of others – as if Caravaggio's collapse on the beach at Porto Ercole and Jarman's succumbing to AIDS several years after he made this film were somehow also a kind of crucifixion. Jarman, it's true, would not learn his HIV status until on 22 December 1986, but it's of course possible that he already suspected he would die 'martyred' by a government unwilling (as it appeared especially in the mid-80s) to spend its resources to conquer a disease whose victims were predominantly society's undesirables (gay men and IV-drug users). We have seen that Jarman liked to speak of Caravaggio as a martyr to religious prejudices against homosexuality. 'The strictures of Church and society' left 'a cancer, a lingering doubt' in this 'most homosexual of painters', and 'in a hostile environment this extreme of self-analysis became self-destruction'. 'All the weight of society' is behind David, who can cut off Goliath–Caravaggio's head 'without a trace of pity'.[29] Not only that: Caravaggio would be destroyed by the object of his desire as well as by the cultural forces hostile to it. He kills his cruel lover, but then carries his portrait with him until his own death. The suffering of the rejected painter is figured in the wistful, 'cruising' glance of his self-portrait in *The Martyrdom of St. Matthew*, which Jarman interpreted as 'martyrdom at the hands of youth' (that 'hero' in the gay bar who won't fuck you…). This is a curious basis for the analogy with Christ's crucifixion; happily, Jarman's film proposes a version of martyrdom more persuasive than the frustration of sexual rejection. It is not so much that Christ's death is *like* Caravaggio's, or that Caravaggio's is *like* Jarman's, but rather that Caravaggio's and Jarman's art *could* substitute one death for the other. The possibility of these substitutions is inherent in the activity of art, and if there is something exhilarating in the imaginary multiplication of identities, there is something terrifying as well. From this perspective, the enacting of analogies – of Caravaggio becoming Christ, of Jarman becoming Caravaggio–Christ – is the source of the artist's martyrdom. And the motivating force behind such identifications may be nothing more than the ease with which they can be aesthetically postulated. The artist is martyred by that ease, martyred not at the hands of youth, but within and by an activity that dissolves and shatters identity. He *is* nowhere and everywhere in his work. It was perhaps at the moment Jarman decided how Caravaggio the boy would be cast and portrayed in the Easter procession sequence that he experienced most directly the power of that activity, a power that could leave him bereft of being.

Christ of course was not martyred by art – or perhaps he was. As an identifiable figure, he is, after all, nothing but centuries of representation, representation (unlike, for example, the sculpted heads of Roman emperors) without a model. His appearance, once conventionalized, became recognizable in art, but it is never repeated in exactly the same manner, with the result that his multiple presences are identical to an unending disappearance. The identity of Christ is an identity at once exalted and martyred by centuries of representation. The historical Caravaggio is unique in that he seems not only to have known that but also to have wanted to make that knowledge visible in his work. Referring to the scandal provoked by Caravaggio's use of models too easily recognizable *as* models (brought mainly from the streets of Rome into the painter's studio), we spoke of the resistance of those models' bodies to a veritable industry of symbolization. They refuse to be seen through, but in emphasizing their own visibility they are also making Christ or the Virgin *more* visible, visible as whoever represents them. It is as if they were proclaiming that the subject on the other side of their represented bodies is nothing but that: *their bodies*. The models, standing in for figures nowhere else to be found, enact the brute suppression of icons whose glory they have been ordered, and paid, to serve, and whom they replace by their very service. This is certainly a martyrdom more abstract than the bodily suffering of Christ on the cross, although in a way it is even more radical in its consequences. Those consequences were perhaps unintentionally anticipated in the Biblical episode of Mary and Mary Magdalen failing to find Christ in his tomb. Between his crucifixion and his resurrection, he disappears, and we might say that his resurrection in Christian art *is* his disappearance. It is a referential art; but it refers to a body having become a ghost in a 'body' of art that, unlike its inspirational source, enacts the *Dis*incarnation. Was all this familiar to Jarman? He certainly never spoke of martyrdom by art. He did say of Caravaggio that 'he paints with a knife',[30] but characteristically, Jarman makes this remark in a context which makes it clear that the 'revenge' that art became for Caravaggio was directed against the man he unhappily loved and the society that condemned such love. And yet Jarman also seems to have come to the edge of the awareness we are speaking of, to have felt – and fled from – the terror of art. For Jarman – and we wish to reconstruct the logic of his move – his refuge was film. The flight in his case was a flight from painting, an activity he would come back to and leave again (one he would come back to even when he had left it: *Caravaggio*). Film, it appears, was fun: you could even make a film, as he said of *Edward II*, in which 'the boys look good and in the end it's all about fucking'[31] – a far cry from what he weakly but none the less tellingly complained of as the loneliness of painting.

IV

Can film be non-narrative? Jarman's remark that *Caravaggio* was the first of his films in which he had 'bowed to narrative' strongly suggests that he thought it could. And the experience of *Caravaggio* didn't convince him of the inevitability of narrative in film. Several years later, a voice-over at the beginning of *The Garden* promises us 'a journey without direction' – a somewhat mysterious remark given the powerful narrative directionality of that film (it moves inexorably toward the torture and crucifixion of the two young gay Christs). For Jarman, the criterion for the non-narrative appears to have been an explosive discontinuity of images. And it is of course possible to make films consisting of an apparently directionless succession of images. However, Jarman never really gives us that. In *Sebastiane* (1976), *Jubilee* and *The Garden*, for example (notwithstanding the seeming lack of connectedness between particular sequences in the last two of these films), the escalation of violence provides a strong narrative intelligibility: toward the crucifixion scenes in *Sebastiane* and *The Garden*, toward the murder of the boys and the punk women's revenge on the cops in *Jubilee*. *The Angelic Conversation* (1985) is structured by a mythic narrative. The lovers' search for each other and their moves toward an erotic union are presented as a Jungian journey through caves and in barren landscapes that finally leads to a sun-drenched shore and cleansing water in which one of the boys bathes. But even without such conspicuous narrative movements, a certain narrative rhythm is inherent in film's unfolding in time. However repetitive or static a film's images may be, it can't help but *move on.* This inevitability is only partially defeated by Jarman's final film, *Blue*. Visually, the film never moves; it is from beginning to end the same blue surface. However, the voice-overs take up, so to speak, the narrative slack; without necessarily 'going anywhere', the sound-track demands the kind of anticipatory attention narrative expects from us. We can leave a painting and come back to it as often as we like without ever 'missing' anything; indeed, how we understand the painting depends in large measure on the rhythm of attention and distraction with which we look at it and turn away from it. Painting, for all the associative visual clues it provides, is a less coercive correction of our naturally wandering, in a sense even naturally unartistic eye. Figurative painting spatializes narrative coercions, thereby tending to organize the time of our looking at it. Non-figurative painting leaves us freer – which means more at a loss – in determining how to look, whereas however difficult a film may be, it always carries us along. It encourages a perceptual passivity which is crucial to its power. A film makes decisions about what to look at next *for us*; but in thus assuming the burden of perceptual time, it also tyrannizes perception by demanding an unflagging attention. Look away, and you've missed something, and when you come back you won't know how important what you've missed is to what you now see. A total surrender of attention is the price film asks for the precious service it performs: that of briefly relieving us from the burden of using time in order to organize space.

Phenomenologically, film is complicit with the exercise of power, a fact that must be taken into account by any politically ambitious film, any film that would criticize oppressive uses of power. This may involve, as we suggested in our study of Alain Resnais in *Arts of Impoverishment*, a film's blocking of its own resources for controlling our attention. It may inhibit its power to tell us where to look, how to move. Power is never entirely renounced; indeed, the very resistance, on the part of the film-maker, to the narrative power to which we customarily surrender with pleasure, cannot be described as an entirely non-coercive move. It does, however, coerce us into a more active perceptual participation in the film's composition. By failing to make certain narrative connections (that would serve narrative intelligibility), Resnais at least partially renounces the power always available to the film-maker: that of carrying his audience along. More exactly, he invites us to understand the mechanics by which his particular version of carrying along is effected. We must reconstruct those connective moves, and tricks, which narrative realism does everything *not* to foreground. In so doing, we are introduced to the possibility of re-forming our ideas of what constitutes a connection – and ultimately, of revising our imagination of the relational. Narrative's most brilliant trick is to deceive us into thinking that we are not implicated in its compositional moves. Our sense of simply going along with them reinforces a distinction between the viewer and the work, which, while it confers on the work the power to direct our movements, also – and most consequentially – nourishes the viewer's illusion of innocence: power is being exercised out there, by the coercive object of our viewing. Resnais' drawing of his spectators into his films is not only designed to make them participate in the film's associative mobility; it is also a way of destroying the spectators' confidence that the coercions to which they submit are alien to them, are never of their own doing.

In *Night and Fog*, his short 1955 documentary on Nazi concentration camps, Resnais draws our attention to the various procedures by which our looking is being disoriented. The blurring of past and present; the discrepancies between what we see and hear; the ingenuities of Resnais' montage; the failure of the camera's tracking movements to organize the visual field into a narrativizable totality: all this draws our attention to the film's own making, away from its content and toward its aestheticizing devices. The film thus prevents us from giving an account of its subject. It forestalls the comfortable illusion that our relation to the Nazi past can be limited to one of documentary

knowledge. As passive spectators of a more conventional documentary work, we would have been able to feel that our reward for letting the film-maker do all the work, for letting ourselves be carried along by his 'knowledge' of the subject, was our appropriation of the subject, its transfer from the film-maker to us. Resnais' aestheticizing strategies substitute the spectator's implication in Nazism for any such passive appropriation. 'Unable to dissociate what we see from an acute and troubled sense of how our seeing is being disoriented, we are, unexpectedly, in the Nazi past. ... The images, the narrative, and the music of Night and Fog have become part of our perceptual movement, of our perceptual being, now. Far from having to warn us that we may have the same impulses as the Nazis (and that this document is therefore relevant to our own societies), Resnais has made the images of Nazism an active part of our contemporaneity. We move within them easily. The Nazi past is already being repeated inside our sensory collaboration with this film, a collaboration that Resnais encourages us to feel as a kind of self-identification and, consequently, as an inescapable complicity.'[32]

Jarman seems to have had a much simpler, and much more comfortable, view of the relation between power and its victims. Even

The concentration camp latrines in *Night and Fog*

before his reduction of social oppression to the oppression of gays and lesbians, he tended to make overly neat distinctions between the exercise and the suffering of violence. The sound-and-fury of Jarman's conspicuously avant-garde films (in particular, *Jubilee*, *The Last of England* and *The Garden*) at once obscures and testifies to the difficulty he had defining the nature of his interest in motifs of power and violence. He failed, most seriously, to see his own implication in oppressive social violence, thus enclosing himself within the crippling if comfortable identity of the victim. Even before his self-identification as a militant queer, his images of social violence lack any irony about his own distance from those images. We of course don't mean to suggest that there is no difference between oppressors and their victims. We are, however, claiming that any effective resistance to social structures based on the master–slave relation must include a recognition of the universal appeal of power and violence. Revolutionaries who claim themselves immune to that appeal have, notoriously, shown themselves eager to experience the powerful pleasures of power and violence once they pass into positions of control, into the identity of the dominant. The absence of any irony about what might be called his own affective positioning in his critiques of social injustice and violence brings Jarman's work closer to the smug confusions of Oliver Stone and Francis Ford Coppola than to the more reserved confidence with which Resnais and (at least in his non-Maoist work) Jean-Luc Godard take on similar themes.

In an interview given after the completion of *Caravaggio*, Jarman complained of the rigidity of the film's format. He expressed frustration at having had to set up scenes in a more formal manner than usual, and at having made a film more controlled than he would have liked.[33] Certainly, having 'bowed to narrative' for this film, Jarman committed himself to an organization he could easily judge as too rigid and controlled in looking back at his work. The implication is that rigidity and control are *not* characteristic of the non-narrative films. The local chaos in Jarman's films is, however, consistent with a good deal of structural rigidity. The framing devices and the narratively neat escalations of violence we mentioned earlier are not the only signs of

Jarman's firm hold over his material – and his audience. The films are a little like the punks in *Jubilee*: the spontaneity of their random acts of violence is countered – and belied – by their extremely articulate ideas on just about everything. Far from being explosive, the film is weighted down by its intellectualism. The characters – and not only Amyl Nitrate, who actually reads to us from her own writings – hold forth on just about everything 'significant': history, art, reality, the media, love, sex. The noise and violence in the film seem designed to divert us from all the saying (all the opinions to which it is assumed we will assent) – as well as from the rigidity of the film's moral line-ups. There is the injustice and brutality of contemporary England, the desperate, sterile, yet somehow sympathetic violence of the punk reaction against it, and, finally, the gentle purity of Angel and Sphinx, the incestuous brother-couple we see mainly caressing each other in bed and who, predictably, are slaughtered by the police toward the end of the film. 'I love you both,' says Viv (who engages in some aesthetic philosophy), and this island of gay male purity is sharply contrasted not only with the culture that would devastate it but also with the boys' murderous female punk roommates.

Punk torture scene from *Jubilee*

Jarman himself criticized *Jubilee*; he thought the film's characters were no more than 'ciphers'.[34] What we find most troubling about the film is, however, more or less a constant in Jarman's work. Not only do his films have a thematic and narrative rigidity only partially concealed by a superficially open, 'directionless' succession of images; not only does his world tend to be non-problematically polarized between violent oppressors and innocent victims; he also engages in exercises of power not unlike those he thought of himself as exposing and struggling against. Others have noted the coercion and even violence frequently associated with homosexual desire in Jarman's films. In the early *Sebastiane* – except for the idyllic scene of two of the soldiers rather chastely making love in the water – desire seems synonymous with the exercise of power. The camera lingers on the captain's torture of Sebastian, and the final sequence treats us to the lovely Sebastian's body being martyred on the cross, repeatedly pierced by arrows. As we have seen, Michele and Ranuccio's intimacy is initiated, celebrated and ended by episodes of violence. In a somewhat milder vein, a terrorist tries, in drunken impotence, to forcibly fuck a man draped over the British flag in *The*

Sebastian's Passion

Last of England, and even in *The Angelic Conversation* the two men's love-making is preceded by a wrestling scene, in which one of them repeatedly forces the other's arms down onto the bed. The alternative to this is the sappy sentimentality of the two boys in *Jubilee*, and a few sequences worthy of a soft-porn cinema (the mild carrying on in the water from *Jubilee*, the two men sort of having sex on Gaveston's bed at the beginning of *Edward II*, the caresses exchanged by the two male beauties in *The Garden*). In *The Garden*, the absence of any violence between the lovers is, so to speak, compensated for by the astonishing length of the sequence in which they stoically endure torture at the hands of a madly laughing psycho who, to the approval of his goon comrades, smears them with some thick jam-like substance. We are of course not saying that Jarman 'approves' of such scenes (and he did speak of the need to expunge the strong sadomasochistic trait in homosexual art), but such scenes are what his imagination comes up with when it represents homosexual desire. The sentimental images are weak; Jarman's most powerful representations of homosexuality are representations of extreme aggression, of getting beaten or forcibly fucked or tortured.

More telling is the complicity of his cinematic rhythms and structures with the power and the violence his admirers praise him for exposing and attacking. The jerky, fractured sequences of *The Last of England* – its hammering rhythm – complicitously repeats the violence it represents. There is no distance between what Jarman does with his camera and what he condemns our culture for doing to all of us. The hysterical speed of the sequences of *The Last of England* belongs to the violence those sequences represent; it is another enactment of that violence. Of course now *we* are the victims, and we suffer a torture appropriate to cinematic victims. Perhaps the best exercise of power the film-maker can have over his audience – much more satisfying, after all, than narrativizing coercions – is to prevent the audience from seeing his film, even *to blind them*. There are different paths to this goal. The images of *The Last of England* often go by us so fast we almost don't see them. Or the film can more explicitly turn its aggression against us. We have mentioned the curious moment in *Caravaggio* when Michele turns in fury toward the camera, cursing the spectator. Most effectively, we can be literally prevented from seeing. Jarman has a favourite technical trick: shining light into a mirror turned toward the camera, so that our seeing is blocked by an explosion of light. Somewhat less dramatically, objects are blurred by all the shots, throughout Jarman's work, of dancing flames and dissolving figures. Visually inhibiting devices can serve very different purposes. When Resnais frustrates our impulse to move toward his images, he is attacking the epistemological confidence usually encouraged by film. The film-maker's power over the spectator rests on the solid foundation of the promise he appears to be making to the spectator: that of giving him or her the world as an object-representation that can be appropriated. The illusion of knowledge – and the reinforcement of the boundaries separating a knowing subject from the object to be known – is the reward for our willingness to be manipulated by film's coercive narrativity. Resnais, on the other hand, forces us to work along with him, thereby transforming us from a passive, appropriating subject into a *collaborative activity*. Now the world of the film can no longer be seen as an object; the film-maker, his representation, and the spectator are all working together, and in so doing they are discovering and constructing their being *as* that working together, as an incessant compositional and associative activity of which, finally, the film itself is only one episode.

In Godard's *Passion*, a film-maker is attempting to shoot a film that includes *tableaux vivants* of several famous paintings. Jerzy, the director, constantly worries, somewhat comically, about whether or not he's getting the light right, a worry that risks paralysing the progress of his film. In the context of *Godard*'s film, this implicitly raises questions about how film 'illuminates' the real. The frequent misfit between image and sound – dialogue from one scene overlaps into another where it doesn't 'belong' – is a technical variant on a more general blurring of distinctions between the film's 'subjects'. We are always between those subjects – not exactly focusing on the making of the film, or on the factory workers' strike, or on Jerzy's love affairs, but rather moving between the factory,

the studio, the hotel, and, with Jerzy, between two women. The film
never gets the diegetic light right on any of these subjects, but this
apparent failure is the film's major achievement. It makes it impossible
for us to identify, and to mark the boundaries of such activities and
subjects as film-making, factory work and love, thereby proposing a
solidarity of being among these subjects that is a generalized or ideal
configuration of the solidarity supporting the workers' strike. Such
solidarity defeats identification (saying what 'work' is, what 'love' is) –
most importantly, from a political perspective, the identifications that
allow for disciplinary controls over human activities. *Passion* suggests the
limited usefulness of thinking about how the conditions of work might
be changed unless we first of all re-imagine work itself. An impoverished
definition of work necessarily impoverishes projects for reforming those
conditions. Any such re-imagining depends on our relinquishing
definitional certainties: certainties about, for instance, where work ends,
where love begins. To grasp the operative interconnectedness of all our
activities may appear to reduce them to being 'merely' inaccurate

The filming of the film in Godard's *Passion*

replications of one another, but that very sameness liberates each activity from the narrow confines of an individual identity. Universal similitude becomes the ground for universal *exchanges* – exchanges of function, of rhythm, of stress, and of pleasure.

Jerzy's perplexity about what lighting to use for his film is Godard's refusal to illuminate his subjects for us. They aren't clearly separated, they run into each other. But by inhibiting cognitive security in his spectators, Godard, like Resnais, initiates other sorts of movement: not appropriative movements toward his subjects, but rather a kind of circulation within them, a testing of the displaceability of the presumed properties of each activity. The blurring of boundaries works, for the most part, very differently in Jarman. His Turneresque reduction of the visual field to blankets of near whiteness initiates nothing; it ends everything. He blinds us not in order to re-direct us, but as the ultimate nihilistic expression of his directorial power. Jarman's conscious judgment of punk style notwithstanding, most of his work is complicit with the punk nihilism of *Jubilee*. Gaveston is punkism resurrected in Jarman's late work. His vicious mockery of power and his adulation of power are wonderfully expressed when his naked body writhes with deliberate disgust on Edward's throne. Jarman's unintended message that there is no alternative to power (except those wholly unexamined images of sweet gay love) seems to have led to his fascination with a power that can't be resisted, that is, a power that totally destroys. In a sense, the ability of film-makers like Resnais and Godard to propose types of mobility different from the coercive narrative mobility so easily available to them *as* film-makers depends on a certain scepticism about the reality of power. By this we don't mean a scepticism about the historical effects of the exercise of power. That exercise never stops destroying, and it is also true that it never stops meeting resistances (which, as Foucault argued, are also moves of power). But perhaps the pre-condition for truly effective resistances to power is the realization that ontologically, power is an illusion. *Being does not move coercively*. It is a circulation of forms and energies and not an appropriation of objects. Within the appropriative medium of film *Passion* positions its spectators

within that circulation, as if Godard found a certain exhilaration in
working, within film, against the ontology it presupposes.

Perhaps because of this ultimate impotence of power, its nihilistic
manifestation can't help but be something like a desperate cry. Jarman's
films are full of such (frequently silent) cries. We are thinking of the
extraordinary scenes of oral desperation in *The Last of England*: the
naked man gasping repeatedly on a head of raw cauliflower, and the
figure played by Tilda Swinton chewing madly on the wedding dress she
has just torn apart with scissors. These are sequences of psychotic self-
indulgence, of a rare self-exposure. The furiously frustrated orality they
depict may be the most desperate expression of the human psyche. It
brings us back to the horrendous impotence of an abandoned infancy,
and to the murderous fury of that impotence. In his appreciative and
perceptive study of Jarman's films, Michael O'Pray responds to such
scenes with 'a strong sense of Jarman struggling to find images to express
his feelings'.[35] We would be inclined to say, on the contrary, that the
images in the cauliflower and torn dress sequences are not of the sort we

Tilda Swinton in *The Last of England*'s dress-tearing scene

are likely to come up with when we struggle consciously to 'express our feelings', but are rather the sign of an exceptional tapping into unconscious representations. Jarman was very cagey about the subject of *The Last of England* (what it is about *and* its psychic source). As so often in his comments about his work, he seems to know what he has done at the same time that he doesn't want to think too closely about what he has done (he said, astonishingly, that he had made *The Last of England* off the top of his head), and so he gives us a kind of muddled covering of his tracks. He called the film a 'documentary', documentary 'from somewhere far away'. But then it turns out that the far away was also close at hand: 'Everything I pointed the camera at ... had meaning, it didn't matter what we filmed.' In addition, this documentary is a 'fiction', since 'all film is fiction, including the news, or, if you want to reverse it, all film is fact'.[36] In what way, exactly, a documentary is fiction is left unexamined, as is the more fundamental question of the specificity of a documentary fictional film as distinguished from a non-documentary fictional film. Everything, it appears, is everything else, so you can't accuse the film-maker of doing, or not doing, anything.

Jarman did acknowledge that he had put himself 'into the centre of the picture'. The film opens with images of Jarman at his table writing, and home movies from Jarman's comfortable middle-class childhood are juxtaposed with the nightmarish scenes of contemporary urban decay and chaos. *The Last of England*, Jarman wrote, is a 'dream allegory'.[37] An allegory of what? The film has been taken to be a 'critique of British post-imperialism', 'a less personal film ... than it might seem'.[38] But what is the relation between the images of military gangs terrorizing England and the cauliflower and bridal dress sequences? The latter overwhelm us not with their political acumen, but as uncensored fantasmatic confessions. The film is in effect, as Jarman enigmatically said, 'a documentary ... from somewhere far away', the 'far away', we suggest, of great psychic 'distances'. There is in all this a potentially interesting treatment of the difficulty of sustaining a political consciousness, of the problematic nature of our efforts to distinguish perception from fantasy. It's not necessary to think of such a project as discrediting political commitment, but it would bring to such things as 'a critique of British post-imperialism' an ironic sense of the critiquing subject's implication in his images of imperialism. *The Last of England* testifies to Jarman's over-powering fantasmatic invasion of his state-of-the-nation filmic project, at the same time as it implicitly proclaims the documentary nature of the project. Resnais' irony even in a bona fide documentary about Nazi concentration camps, far from being a sign of his political indifference or 'coldness', is a way of acknowledging that his seriousness about his subject cannot be wholly innocent, that he is *in it* in ways he can't entirely control. (And it's that acknowledgment that gives authority to the documentary ambition of *Night and Fog*.) Jarman, it could be argued, makes the same demonstration in *The Last of England*, but it is a demonstration made, as it were, without his consent. Unwilling to inject any irony into his images of violent excess (and excessive violence) in British society, he ends up being everywhere in them, leaving no space at all for a convincing political critique. His inclusion of images of himself at his writing table and in the movies from his childhood is his indecisive way of announcing his presence in the film. But those scenes are clearly detached from the rest, they don't acknowledge the subjective presence permeating the entire film. The only refuge from the all invasive violence of *The Last of England* – the social violence it depicts, the desperate violence of psychotic impotence, the violent hammering rhythm with which the film assaults its audience – is the nostalgia for family (and perhaps even Empire, the Empire briefly figured in ambiguous, rhythmically seductive marching sequences…).

Curiously, Jarman seems to have taken great emotional comfort in making this truly frightening film. Asked in the context of a discussion of *The Last of England* why he made films, he answered: 'For the camaraderie.'[39] Referring in *Dancing Ledge* to his work in the theatre room at the Slade, Jarman wrote: 'I like working on shared projects. It breaks down the isolation of working as a painter.' And, referring in the same autobiographical text to the way in which his collaboration as set designer in Ken Russell's *The Devils* usurped his life during almost every waking moment of 1970, Jarman confessed: 'Painting was the major victim: I continued it over the next ten years very sporadically. After the intense pressure under which a film is made, it seemed undemanding – and the isolation in which it was pursued, enervating.'[40] The *Caravaggio* script picks up this motif of the painter's isolation, making it part of Jarman's portrait of Michele. The script includes a voice-over only partly used in the film in which Michele refers to Jerusaleme as 'a companion in my loneliness – nothing can come about without loneliness and I have created a loneliness for myself that no one can imagine'. Later in the film, toward the end of the party in the Catacombs, the painter watches his model Pipo dance with a handsome young man; he blows them a kiss, smiles, and then (although this is not exactly how Terry played the scene) 'his face goes blank with loneliness'. It's immediately after this that Michele returns to his studio where he sees Jerusaleme asleep on the dais wearing Ranuccio's cloak from *St. John the Baptist*. Surveying his assistant and the empty studio, Caravaggio says: 'You are my St. John and this is our Wilderness.'[41]

Painting substitutes for the narrative movement of film a *now* that will not necessarily be followed. Not being immersed in a temporary flow that stops only with the film's ending, both the painter and his spectators can repeatedly turn away from and return to the work. The absence of narrative coercion invites, could even be felt as demanding, the exploration of other types of movement and connectedness. Was film in part a flight from such demands? Film seems to have allowed Jarman to experience the pleasure of being carried along – both by the conviviality on the set and the rhythm of the production. Curiously, however, it was not an escape from what could be imagined as the private terrors associated with solitude. Indeed, the powerful narrative momentum of a film allowed for the deployment of those terrors – as if Jarman could escape being overwhelmed by fantasmatic chaos and violence only if they were inserted within, and contained by, the disciplinary frames and temporal framework of film. Painting, on the other hand, was accompanied by a melancholy that perhaps both announced and kept suppressed the menace of disintegration. The painter's loneliness designates not only the absence of company, but, more frighteningly, the

always imminent loss of self. There are interesting moments in *Caravaggio* of a pregnant loneliness – one that might give birth to new relations, in particular relations not constricted by desire. These moments are all connected to painting. Relaxing one afternoon from his work on *Profane Love*, Michele shares with Pipo what Jarman calls in the script 'a moment of heightened awareness'. Michele watches Pipo perform some languid gymnastics, after which the two look at each other 'wistfully'.[42] It is a curiously still moment; something is exchanged, without their moving toward each other, but we don't know what. There is a similar wistfulness in Michele's relation to Jerusaleme; it is most effectively expressed both in the early scene when, having just brought the boy back to his studio, Michele gathers him up onto his lap and silently holds him, and in the studio scene referred to a moment ago when Michele addresses the sleeping Jerusaleme as 'my St. John'. The studio is their wilderness; cut off from everyone else, they may, like St. John and Christ, announce and bring into the world something unprecedented. What that might be is by no means clear, but each time it is evoked the painter's work is emphasized. The most mysterious example of this is a sequence in which the camera moves from Jerusaleme crushing lemon juice into his mouth to a table covered with Michele's painting materials (brushes,

Michele wistfully watches Pipo

flasks of oil, the slab for grinding the paints) and finally to a large Bible from which Michele reads aloud. The passage is from the *Song of Songs*; it is a lament of unanswered desire:

> Upon my bed at night
> I sought him whom my soul loves
> I sought him but found him not
> I called him but he gave no answer.
> I will rise now and go about the city.
> In the street and the squares
> I will seek him whom my soul loves.
> I sought him but found him not.

If the lover is not found, what else might there be? In the three sequences just looked at, Jarman (somewhat inconclusively, it's true) associates painting both with aborted desire and a non-desiring exchange. The association, largely unexplored, is established mainly through contiguity: the painting materials next to the Bible from which Michele reads, Pipo and Michele exchanging a glance next to the Cupid painting on which they've just been working, Michele addressing

Michele holds the boy Jerusaleme

Jerusaleme dressed as St. John and, in the earlier scene, holding the boy who has just run around the studio using the Medusa-head painting as a shield. However undeveloped, these scenes interestingly suggest that through painting, Michele – and Jarman – discover a connectedness independent of desire. In Jarman, homosexual desire, when it is not violent (as in *Sebastiane* and *Caravaggio*), is represented as little more than attractive male bodies entwined in a comparatively chaste embrace. Might Jarman have seen in Caravaggio other relational possibilities? We speak in *Caravaggio's Secrets* of a non-erotic sensuality in the painter's work. We set this against the early portraits of erotically provocative poses and looks in young men. Our analysis of a tension between a recognizably erotic invitation and self-concealing movements of retreat in these portraits leads us to conclude that they represent an enigmatic address, one that solicits intimacy in order to block it with a secret. Using psychoanalytic categories recently proposed by Jean Laplanche, we trace the genealogy of that address to a relation that inaugurates sexuality in the human subject. The inability to decipher the 'enigmatic signifier' (Laplanche's term for an adult world infiltrated with unconscious and sexual significations and messages by which the child is seduced but which the child can't understand) constitutes us as sexual beings, that is, beings in whom desire or lack is central. Desire *as* lack is born, we argue, as the exciting pain of a certain ignorance: the failure to penetrate the sense of the other's soliciting – through touch, voice, gesture or look – of our body. The enigmatic signifier narrows and centres our look; it is the originating model of a relationality in which subject and object are separated by the distance of an imaginary secret or a special authority, a distance that only 'knowledge' might cross or eliminate. This is, however, the mode of address *against* which Caravaggio's most original paintings work. Like all painting, his work is about forms of connectedness in space, and, most notably in such works as the Capitolino Museum's *Fortune Teller* and *St. John the Baptist with a Ram*, he experiments with a gaze diverted from a space circumscribed by the mutual and paranoid fascination of imaginary secrets. We study the non-erotic sensuality of these works as an unmappable extensibility of being. If we still have 'secrets', they are now secrets not of interiority but rather of untraceable spatial disseminations; if there is still 'concealment', it is the concealment of a visibility beyond the painting to which the painting directs us.

Desire produces voids. It violates the ontology to which Caravaggio's work directs us: everything connects to and within the wholeness of being. In his paintings, Caravaggio outlines for us an aesthetic that may owe nothing to sacrifice (in psychoanalytic terms, to the 'authorized' violence of castration), that may be identical to a total acceptance and even, in art, to any implicit sanctification of all space. We are of course not saying that Jarman 'saw all this' in Caravaggio. He did, however, live for several years in an exceptional closeness to his subject's work. And his film reveals an attention and an intimacy far more impressive than the crude analogy between *The Martyrdom of St. Matthew* and a night of sexual frustration in a gay bar. There are those slight differences between Caravaggio's paintings and their reproductions (on canvas, and especially in the models' poses) in the film which, far from indicating any lack of care in Jarman's looking at the paintings, are actually the signs of his profound attention and attachment. As we argued earlier, this sense of the paintings' power is so acute that he not only imagines them to have 'instigated' a life but is also compelled partially to 'correct' the paintings so that their effect on the painter's life may be retroactively included within them. Furthermore, the film is saturated, in discreetly inventive ways, with references to paintings that, unlike *The Martyrdom of St. Matthew* and *The Death of the Virgin*, are not dramatically centred. A few examples: In an early scene, Jerusaleme, in a moment reminiscent of *St. John the Baptist with a Ram* (1602), is caressing a ram in the studio; during the painting of *The Martyrdom of St. Matthew*, there is a reference to the painter's self-portrait when Michele looks over his shoulder at Ranuccio posing as the executioner; the brief scene in which Davide touches Michele's wound from the knife fight with Ranuccio evokes Caravaggio's *Doubting Thomas*. More generally, like Caravaggio's paintings (nearly devoid of landscape), Jarman's film, shot within the docklands warehouse, has (with the exception of Lena's corpse floating on water – the Thames) only the lighting of an indoor studio. In the

The lovers of *The Angelic Conversation*

Davide-Doubting Thomas touching Michele-Christ's wound

annotated script, Jarman speaks of the care with which he and his crew (especially the cameraman, Gabriel Beristain) chose the colours of the film:

the exact shade of white for the death-bed scenes in Porto Ercole; the warm grey of the studio which was matched to the background of the painting of the Magdalen; pale greens and yellows for the sequences of Caravaggio's youth where the light is luminous and devoid of shadows; the predominant colour a golden yellow (Naples yellow), the background of the still-lifes and simple genre paintings of his formative years. The subjects of these paintings reflected a lightness of touch, music, cardsharping, fortune telling. We decided the film would start in the same way and follow the painter's descent into the dark shadows.

'I have tried', Jarman also writes, 'to create every aspect of the film in the ambience of the paintings.' What he calls 'the visual grammar of the film' was vital: 'a blue globe, the only blue in the film – Caravaggio said "blue is poison" – is balanced perfectly by a blue pot in *Profane Love*; the camera pans across our still lifes only once to reveal the studio table, the work bench; the ivy crown of *The Sick Bacchus* is echoed by the gold crown with which the Cardinal replaces it. Small gestures; but nothing is left to chance.'[43]

The London warehouse became, then, the aesthetic wilderness in which, we might say, Jarman heard Carvaggio's biography being dictated to him from his own absorption in the paintings. With *Caravaggio*, something of the loneliness Jarman associated with painting couldn't help but find its way into film. There is not only the represented loneliness of Michele himself; speaking of the difficulty of cinematically framing the paintings, Jarman also notes: 'Embalmed in films, the paintings look desperately lonely.'[44] It is, however, at these moments of loneliness and, as we have noted, always in conjunction with a painting, that we see Michele not entirely alone, but rather wistfully suspended between a total isolation and the agitation of his desire for Ranuccio. In that suspension, other relational lines at least begin to be drawn: to Pipo, to Jerusaleme, Michele's St. John who, like painting, is mute. Nothing much is explicitly made of these moments, but in the context of the film's images of annihilating desire (both homosexual and heterosexual: Michele and Ranuccio, Ranuccio and Lena), they resonate in a manner incommensurate with the meagre attention given to them. Their suggestiveness is even greater if we think of them in the context of Jarman's other films. The oral rapacity in the scenes discussed earlier from *The Last of England* could be seen as a desperate response to the voids produced by desire. Desire imprisoned in lack avenges itself by a furious incorporation of objects, an attempt literally to stuff the hole of desiring being. Nothing less than psychic survival may depend on imagining those other relational lines.

There are moments in Jarman's work when a sort of non-desiring connectedness is shown even in homosexual love. We are thinking, for example, of the sequence in *The Angelic Conversation* in which, the two lovers having finally found each other, one repeatedly leans over to kiss the other lying (perhaps sleeping) next to him. The scene has neither erotic intensity nor erotic languor. (There are several images of the latter in Jarman's films: Angel and Sphynx in bed in *Jubilee*, the swimming scene in *Sebastiane*, the lovers embracing in a tub in *The Garden*.) The repetition and the lack of response from the boy being kissed de-eroticize the scene; it becomes an image of tenderness at once de-sexualized and de-psychologized, expressed entirely as a certain kind of movement, the particular 'line' of one body reaching toward another. The rhythm of this movement (if not its exact shape) is repeated at the end of the film, when one of the boys leans forward slightly to kiss a flower he brings several times to his lips. Tenderness between humans is thus represented as one moment, one version of a 'reaching toward the other' in space. Tenderness *is* that movement; it escapes the violence of human desire by enacting its independence from either the demands or the presumed secrets of subjectivity. Because of subjectivity, however, tenderness is a difficult form of contact for human subjects. It may, Jarman also suggests, depend on a certain degree of self-recognition in the object we reach toward. The two boys resemble one another, and in a scene shortly before their coming together, one of them presses his face against a mirror, kissing his image. The narcissism represented here facilitates contacts with the world rather than imprisoning the subject in solipsistic relations to others. Given the film's emphasis on various forms of movement toward others – the journey toward the lover, the human and the non-human objects of tenderness, the frequent dissolves from one identity to another – what might have been seen as a specular narcissism should rather be read as the subject's recognition that in approaching otherness, he is also moving toward himself. A non-antagonistic relation to difference depends on this inaccurate replication of the self *in* difference, on our recognizing that *we are already out there*. Self-love initiates the love of others; the love of the same does not erase difference when it takes place as a dismissal of the prejudicial opposition between sameness and difference. Difference can then be loved as a non-threatening supplement to sameness.[45] The dominant photographic techniques of *The Angelic Conversation* were significantly different from those of *The Last of England*. Whereas the hysterical speed of the latter film furiously assaults vision itself (that is, the very perception of the urgent message about cultural decay), the slow motion and freeze-frame techniques of *The Angelic Conversation* are a way of evoking our perceptual care, the care necessary to see each instant *now* (as we might in a painting…), as it reveals itself to us, unprotected, *as it is*.

It was difficult for Jarman to imagine such contacts. Violence may have been the form of connectedness most readily available to his visual imagination. This would explain the great appeal of quiet, even of stasis, in his work and in his life. For all the queer militancy of his final years, Jarman never presented himself as a revolutionary agitator. He consistently expressed his nostalgia for the stability of lost values. An interview published in 1991 is especially clear about how he wished to be thought of politically:

I am not an outsider. The one thing I really regret about my career was that I was put into the position of being anything but the most traditional film-maker of my generation. I hope this has not disappointed you, but this is what I really wanted and that's why I did *The Tempest*, which was a passion for me and which deals with and upholds traditional strands of the culture. Yet I was made into a fake revolutionary. The older I get, the more I believe in tradition. The tradition of hedgerows and fields with flowers – in opposition to the commercialization or the destruction and rape of the countryside and cities.[46]

Contemporary life, Jarman felt, made impossible the unthreatened durability of the cultural forms he longed for, a longing he never disguised. His personal version of the calm and reliable repetitions no longer politically available was undoubtedly his garden at Dungeness. *Derek Jarman's Garden* is one of his most beautiful works, both for the loving detail with which Jarman describes the cultivation of his exceptionally rich garden, and for the subtle suggestions within the writing of a quiet without language, of the kind of contemplative stillness he enjoyed when, as he tells us, he would look peacefully at one plant for an hour. Indeed, the most effective – and extreme – escape from social chaos as well as from a fantasmatic 'commitment' to violent desire as the privileged form of human contact is a transcendence of the very conditions of human life. That move is nearly made (it can never be entirely realized within a human work) in the remarkable film *Blue*. Visually, the film is seventy-five minutes of a slightly pulsing but otherwise unchanging blue. What we described as an inescapable condition of film is transcended: we can look away without missing anything. It's true that the accompanying voice-overs orchestrate a narrative accompaniment. With the four voices of John Quentin, Nigel Terry, Jarman and Tilda Swinton, with Simon Fisher Turner's music, and with the account of Jarman's AIDS symptoms and the painful treatments he underwent, the film can hardly be said to be without narrativizing differentiations. But the voices themselves often bring us back to the unchanging images, enlisting sound in the service of a monotonous, transcendent silence: 'In the pandemonium of image / I present you with the universal Blue / Blue an open door to soul / An infinite possibility / Becoming tangible.' Blue is the colour without 'boundaries or solutions'.

It is the after-image of the shattering bright light of the eye specialist's camera, an image that leads Jarman beyond images. The vicissitudes of HIV-infection become the empirical path to transcendence – through death, of course, but also to a kind of liberating spirituality in life. Jarman quotes the Biblical command, Thou shalt not create unto thyself any graven image, appropriating it for one of his most profound needs: 'to be released from image'.[47]

This extraordinary wish on the part of a painter and film-maker is one of the most impressive, and desolate, aspects of Jarman's work. He projected that wish onto another painter: Caravaggio. 'I've trapped pure spirit in matter,' Michele boasts as he feverishly paints *Death of the Virgin*. Religion is corrupt ('what should grow like the lilies of the field is horribly perverted, placed high on the altars of Rome in mockery'); spirit seeks refuge in art. Is Michele saying that spirit is visible in the matter of painting, or is it hidden there? Earlier he had spoken of 'thought without image lost in the pigment', and just before the shot of Michele working on the *Death of the Virgin* painting, we have heard him evoke some space of utter darkness, 'beyond matter', as he cradles Lena's corpse – the dead Virgin – in his arms:

Michele painting *Death of the Virgin*

Look! Look! Alone again. Down into the back of the skull. Imagining and dreaming, and beyond the edge of the frame – darkness. The black night invading. The soot from the candles darkening the varnish, creeping round the empty studio, wreathing the wounded paintings, smudging out in the twilight – sharp knife-wounds that stab you in the groin, so you gasp and gulp the air, tearing your last breath from the stars as the seed runs into parched sheets and you fall into the night. I float on the glassy surface of the still dark lake, lamp-black in the night, silent as an echo; a mote in your eyes, you blink and send me spinning, swallowed in the vortex. I shoot through the violent depths. The unutterable silence of these waters. A tear forms and drops. The ripples spread out beyond the furthest horizon. Beyond matter, scintilla, star, I love you more than my eyes.

In *Caravaggio*, transcendence is downward; it is identical to drowning. In this powerful scene, Michele traces a passage from the violence of sex to the 'unutterable silence' of death in water. Ejaculation into the 'parched sheets' is accompanied by a painful 'last breath'; it is like 'sharp knife-wounds in the groin'. A fatal orgasm wounds the groin just as Caravaggio had 'wounded' his canvases by painting on them with his knife – as if the process of trapping pure spirit in his art had repeatedly rehearsed a violent death caused by consummated desire. Consummated, not frustrated: Jarman's critical statements about Michele's unrequited love for Ranuccio-the-executioner are a shockingly banal reading of his own film compared to this acknowledgment of the incompatibility of existence and *jouissance*. Sexuality is the self-lacerating passage from life to death, from images of phenomena to 'pure spirit' hidden in art – and, finally, from homosexual to heterosexual love. Orgasm takes place between men (elsewhere Michele remembers masturbating Pasqualone), but it propels Michele into blinding intimacy with the woman. This other love – the love 'beyond matter, scintilla, star' – is without seeing; indeed, it supersedes seeing ('I love you more than my eyes'), which of course means that it supersedes Michele's art. It is the pure spirit of painting, finally released from the images of painting; the 'thought' that comes with obliteration, nothingness.

'Where is the feminine in *The Last of England*?' Jarman asks in *Kicking the Pricks*: 'Until Tilda takes over the film in its last minutes, it is represented by my mother, Elizabeth Evelyn … Tilda, blown by a whirlwind of destruction, becomes a figure of strength … She projects and protects love's idyll, a mother, my mother.'[48] There is no 'love's idyll' for Lena to protect in *Caravaggio*, and Michele's relation to her includes the erotic intensity of that moment when they passionately kiss, watched by a sullen, abandoned Ranuccio. But she of course does become a mother – Christ's mother and, as the substitution of Michele's head for Christ's in *The Entombment* scene indicates clearly enough, the painter's mother – but the 'protection' she offers is a watery union in death. This peculiar version of transcendence, a drowning away from life that is a sinking below images into undifferentiated darkness, is pointed to from the very beginning when Jarman modifies Baglione's account of Caravaggio's death at Porto Ercole (quoted in the script) so that the painter will have died by drowning: 'Rough hands warm my dying body, snatched from the cold blue sea.' Soon after this the memory of sinking to the bottom of the sea near Porto Ercole is merged with a memory of Pasqualone from Michele's childhood: '[Pasqualone's] hand parting my hair like the ripples at the bottom of the ocean.' Finally, just before dying, Michele imagines the wooden bed on which he is lying as 'the barque that bears me across the ocean of night. I bury my head in the pillow and dream of my true love, Pasqualone. I am rowing to you on the great dark ocean.' But this final nostalgic gesture toward Pasqualone (never present in the film as an object of desire) is far less resonant than Michele's posthumous love for Lena-the-Virgin-Mother. Still alive, he sees the 'black night' of his death, his own body floating 'on the glassy surface of the still-dark lake', as he cradles Lena's corpse. Floating, and then spinning. In his final address to Lena's dead body, Michele illuminates the sense toward which, we should now realize, all the images of circling in the film have been moving. Jerusaleme running around Michele's studio holding the Medusa shield, the young Michele literally leading the hustled Englishman around in circles, the horse being led in circles during the New Year's Eve celebration in Michele's studio (while

Jerusaleme waves a red flag in circular motion), Pipo's circling dance at the Catacombs party: Michele's hallucinatory anticipation of his own death as a 'spinning' dramatically concludes this series of rotating movements in *Caravaggio*. The painter imagines himself 'swallowed in the vortex'; he 'shoot[s] through the violet depths'. The ultimate 'wounded rotation' – to borrow a striking phrase from Timothy Murray's perceptive analysis of this motif in *Caravaggio*[49] – is a 'return', in death, to the intra-uterine immersion in liquid which originally nourished us into life and which has now become a death shared with the mother in a devouring vortex.

We should perhaps be more indulgent than we have been toward such sugary scenes as Angel and Sphynx smooching in bed or the two boys lying together in a tub in *The Garden*. They are Jarman's last resort, buffeted as he seems to have been fantasmatically between the cruelty and violence of homosexual desire and a hunger for the mother so insatiable and so desperate that it can be satisfied only by a posthumous return to the union before birth, or rather by a posthumous revision of that union in which, no longer a promise of life, it is re-lived as a

New Year's Eve, 1600

drowning love with, and within, her. Thus in Jarman's cinematic biography of 'the most homosexual of painters', the ultimate 'truth' of homosexuality is represented as an inconsolable heterosexuality. There is no dissociating the homosexual from the heterosexual in *Caravaggio*, not because Jarman buys into the fashionable distaste for such 'essentializing' labels, but rather because he shows us the heterosexual emerging from *within* the homosexual. The relation between Michele and Ranuccio reveals itself to be a rivalry for Lena's love.[50] Psychoanalytically, the film proposes a modification of the classic view of homosexual desire as deriving from an Oedipal configuration in which the boy's primary love is for the father and the mother is in the position of the rival. *Caravaggio* suggests that the boy's rival *is always the father*, and that homosexual desire is, first of all, the erotically inflected persistence of that rivalry and, profoundly and paradoxically, the militantly heterosexual refusal to renounce the mother as an object of desire. The rival's death does not, however, make the mother available to the son. Indeed, *Caravaggio* suggests that the Oedipal structure itself merely 'rationalizes' an earlier experience of the mother's inaccessibility. The boy had already lost her before the father demanded that he give her up. And his loss was inscribed in his desire; it was the *sense of his desire*. He desired her 'released from [her] image', beyond all seeing. This is a heterosexual desire which no condition in life could ever satisfy; it is therefore inconsolable before it is frustrated or forbidden.

Caravaggio, it could be said, gives us a naked psyche; it is the complete unveiling of that psyche. This is its impressive achievement and yet, if that were the final word about it, it would also define its limitations. Jarman's art, at its highest, would be an art of *exposure*. He would have brilliantly orchestrated the cinematic metaphors that illuminate an inner constellation, the constellation that is his self-characterizing memory of desire. In this work, however, Jarman also does something else: he pressures the psychological *ex*posure into becoming an ontological *dis*closure. He does this by pushing the desiring subject, as well as the objects of his desire, toward the unidentifiable. The sequences of Michele cradling Lena, of the *Entombment*, and of

Michele's death at once condense and disperse signification. Lena the dead prostitute is also the dead Virgin, and Michele's head replaces Christ's head in the *Entombment* scene. Thus Michele cradling Lena is also Christ holding his dead mother; it further evokes and reverses the more familiar image of the Virgin mourning her son (frequently figured in painting as Mary holding the crucified Jesus in her lap). The film begins with another scene of mourning: Jersualeme's mother weeping as Caravaggio–Christ takes away Jerusaleme–St. John the Baptist, takes him away to prepare (the materials) for the painter's, the savior's, redemptive work. Also, the crucified Christ is Jarman martyred by his disease and by homophobic hostility and neglect, and Jarman is Christ martyred by all the simulacra of art. The beloved Davide of Jarman's boyhood becomes Michele's occasional lover, and the figure corresponding to that early love is named Pasqualone, the historical Caravaggio's rival for Lena's favours. These slippages of identity from one body to another, this interchangeability of being, help us to re-define homosexuality: no longer

Jerusaleme takes leave of his grandmother

(merely) a particular sexual orientation, it can be seen as the sexuality most appropriate to a perceived solidarity of being in the universe. Identities are never individual; homosexual desire is a reaching out toward an *other sameness*. Homosexuality *expresses* a homoness that vastly exceeds it but that it none the less has the privilege, and the responsibility, of making visible.

From this perspective, the final scenes of *Caravaggio* are celebratory rather than scenes of mourning. They give us Michele, Caravaggio, Jarman continuing beyond the limits of their particular forms. The replicability of being gives rise to an expansive rather than a self-enclosing narcissism, one far removed from the victimized narcissism of much of Jarman's other work. We can now see one of the most disastrous consequences of his queer victim-pride: it plays into the hands of his (of our) oppressors by making him (us) eminently identifiable, imprisoning us within a persecuted identity. Giving in to a temptation

Raising the cross in *The Garden*

perhaps common to all victims – that of making their victimization the ground of their proclaimed superiority – the cover-boy martyrs of *The Garden* become excessively visible in their proud and damaged prettiness. *Caravaggio* emphasizes the ontological dignity of an uncertain or fleeting visibility, of pushing beyond our form in order to circulate within universal similitudes. It is a dignity to which, as *Caravaggio* also emphasizes, art gives us access. In identifying himself with Caravaggio's identification with Christ, Jarman submitted to the beneficent martyrdom of art. Only that submission, that surrender, might have appeased the mad hunger of the cauliflower-devourer in *The Last of England,* for it would have revealed a suffering (a loss of self) exactly identical to a potentially ecstatic Passion, that of self-dispersion. *Caravaggio* entombs that nakedly anxious self, resurrecting it, transformed, as ontological disclosure, as uncircumscribable reappearances within the plenitude of Being.

Notes

1 Derek Jarman, *Dancing Ledge* (Woodstock, New York: The Overlook Press, 1984 [1993]), pp. 9–10.

2 Derek Jarman, *Derek Jarman's Caravaggio*, with special photography by Gerald Incandela (London: Thames and Hudson, 1986), p. 44.

3 Jarman, *Caravaggio*, p. 44.

4 See Leo Bersani and Ulysse Dutoit, *Caravaggio's Secrets* (Cambridge, Mass.: Harvard University Press, 1998), pp. 46–7.

5 Jarman, *Dancing Ledge*, pp. 21–2, 24. A principal object of Jarman's later struggles against homophobic public policy, the infamous Clause 28 of the 1988 Local Government Act reads as follows:

1. A local authority shall not:
   (a) Intentionally promote homosexuality or publish material with the intention of promoting homosexuality.
   (b) Promote the teaching in any maintained school of the acceptability of homosexuality as a pretended family relationship.
2. Nothing in sub-section 1 shall be taken to prohibit the doing of anything for the purpose of treating or preventing the spread of disease.
3. In any proceedings in connection with the application of this section, a court shall draw such inferences as to the motivation of the local authority as may reasonably be drawn from the evidence before it.

6 Jarman, *Dancing Ledge*, pp. 22, 13.

7 *By Angels Driven: The Films of Derek Jarman*, ed. Chris Lippard (Westport, Conn.: Greenwood Press, 1996), pp. 7, 12–13, 51, 120–1, 84.

8 James Brooke, 'Gay Man Beaten and Left for Dead; 2 are Charged', *The New York Times*, 12 October 1998, p. A10.

9 Derek Jarman, *Queer Edward II* (London: British Film Institute, 1991), p. 26.

10 David Hawkes, '"The Shadow of this time": the Renaissance Cinema of Derek Jarman', in *By Angels Driven*, pp. 110–11.

11 The historical Gaveston was in fact a scion of Gascon nobility.

12 Jarman, *Queer Edward II*, p. 20.

13 Jarman, *Kicking the Pricks* (Woodstock, New York: The Overlook Press, 1997), p. 122.

14 Jarman, *Dancing Ledge*, p. 22.

15 Jarman, *Caravaggio,* p. 6.

16 Jarman, *Dancing Ledge*, pp. 14, 18, 24, 26.

17 Ibid., p. 14.

18 Jarman, *Caravaggio,* p. 48.

19 Ibid., p. 121.

20 Jarman, *Dancing Ledge*, p. 24.

21 Ibid., pp. 24, 13.

22 Jarman, *Caravaggio*, p. 133.

23 The criminal complaint filed against Caravaggio is summarized by Howard Hibbard in his *Caravaggio* (New York: Harper and Row, 1983), p. 191.

24 Jarman, *At Your Own Risk: A Saint's Testament* (Woodstock, New York: Overlook Press, 1992), p. 15.

25 Jarman, *Caravaggio,* p. 10.

26 Ibid., p. 52.

27 Ibid., pp. 101–2, 52.

28 Ibid., p. 118.

29 Jarman, *Dancing Ledge*, p. 22.

30 Ibid., p. 24.

31 Jarman, *Queer Edward II*, p. 126.

32 Leo Bersani and Ulysse Dutoit, *Arts of Impoverishment: Beckett, Rothko, Resnais* (Cambridge, Mass.: Harvard University Press, 1993), p. 187.

33 Interview with Michael O'Pray, 'Brittania on Trial', in *Monthly Film Bulletin* vol. 53 no. 627, April 1986.

34 Jarman, *Caravaggio*, p. 132.
35 Michael O'Pray, *Derek Jarman: Dreams of England* (London: British Film Institute, 1996), p. 159.
36 Jarman, *Kicking the Pricks*, p. 170.
37 Ibid., p. 188.
38 O'Pray, *Derek Jarman*, p. 156; Annette Kuhn, *Family Secrets: Acts of Memory and Imagination* (London: Verso, 1995), p. 109. Chris Lippard and Guy Johnson speak of *The Last of England* as an 'energetic and positive diagnosis of a nation under the malaise of eight years of Thatcher government'. 'Private Practice, Public Health: the Politics of Sickness and the Films of Derek Jarman', in *Fires were Started: British Cinema and Thatcherism*, ed. Lester Friedman (Minneapolis: University of Minnesota Press, 1993), p. 285.
39 Jarman, *Kicking the Pricks*, p. 163.
40 Jarman, *Dancing Ledge*, pp. 74, 105.
41 Jarman, *Caravaggio*, pp. 13, 91, 92.
42 Ibid., p. 75. Timothy Murry writes very interestingly about the importance of a 'stilled wistfulness' in *Caravaggio*, the wistfulness of 'unfulfilled passivity' with 'hallucinatory echoes of the missed encounter'. *Like a Film: Ideological Fantasy on Screen, Camera and Canvas* (London: Routledge, 1993), pp. 158 and 165.
43 Jarman, *Caravaggio*, pp. 22, 94.
44 Ibid., p. 34.
45 This argument is elaborated in Bersani's *Homos* (Cambridge, Mass.: Harvard University Press, 1995).
46 Discussion with Jarman, in *Take Ten: Contemporary British Film Directors*, ed. Jonathan Hacker and David Price (Oxford: Clarendon Press, 1991), p. 255.
47 Jarman, *Blue* (Woodstock, New York: The Overlook Press, 1994), pp. 11, 16, 15.

48 Jarman, *Kicking the Pricks*, p. 203.
49 See Murray, *Like a Film*, pp. 155–8.
50 Rivalry for Lena is obliquely emphasized by Jarman's giving the name of the historical Caravaggio's rival for her favours to his childhood love: Pasqualone.

Credits

CARAVAGGIO

UK
1986

Director
Derek Jarman
Producer
Sarah Radclyffe
Screenplay
Derek Jarman
Based on an original idea
by Nicholas Ward-Jackson
Director of Photography
Gabriel Beristain
Edited by
George Akers
Production Design
Christopher Hobbs
Music
Simon Fisher Turner,
assisted by Mary Phillips

©Derek Jarman
Production Companies
The British Film Institute
presents in association with
Nicholas Ward-Jackson
a B.F.I. production in
association with Channel
Four Television
a film by Derek Jarman
Executive Producer
Colin MacCabe
**Executive in Charge of
Production**
Jill Pack
Production Manager
Sarah Wilson
Project Development
James MacKay

Production Accountant
Sheryl Leonardo
Production Assistant
Jules Bradbury
Runners
Yvonne Little,
Simon Wallace
1st Assistant Director
Glynn Purcell
2nd Assistant Director
Simon Mosely
3rd Assistant Director
Patricia Aldersley
Continuity
Heather Storr
Casting
Debbie McWilliams
Extras Casting
Simon Turner
2nd Camera Operator
Steve Tickner
2nd Camera Assistant
Phil Bough
Focus Puller
Noel Balbirnie
Clapper Loader
John Mathieson
**Camera Department
Trainee**
Mike Barker
Grip
Tony Haughey
Gaffer
Larry Prinz
Sparks
Mickey Donovan, Tony Hare
Floor Runners
Belinda Bemrose,
Luke Losey
Stills
Mike Laye

Assistant Editors
Nicola Black, Anuree De
Silva, Matthew Whiteman,
Alistair Bates
Art Director
Mike Buchanan
Paintings
Christopher Hobbs
Scenic Artists
Annie La Paz, Lucy
Morahan
Construction
'Constructivist', Alistair Gow,
Susan McLenachan,
Robin Thistlethwaite
Runners
Josh Jones, Charlie
McGrigor
Property Master
Tim Youngman
Stagehand
Mark Russo
Costume Designer
Sandy Powell
Wardrobe Supervisor
Annie Symons
Runner
Karen Sherwin
Make-up Artist
Morag Ross
Make-up Assistant
Miri Ben-Shlomo
Titles
Frameline
Musicians
Bill Badley, Steart
Butterfield, Lol Coxhill,
Charlie Duncan, Brian
Gulland, Stuart Hall, Julia
Hodgson, Timothy Hugh,
Neil Kelly, Chi Chi Nwanoku,

Jocelyn Pook, Rodney Skeaping, El Tito, Veryan Weston

Singers
John Douglas-Williams, Charles Gibbs, Mary Phillips, Nicolas Robertson, Angus Smith

Additional Music
'Missa Lux et Orgio', Sicilian work songs, 'El Nino'

Music Engineer
Richard Preston

Sound Recordist
Billy McCarthy

Dubbing Mixer
Peter Maxwell

Dubbing Editor
'Budge' Tremlett

Sound Effects
Studio Sound (Italy)

Boom Swinger
George Richards

Sound Department Trainee
June Prinz

Footsteps
Beryl Mortimer, Ted Swanscott

Deaf and Dumb Teacher
Paul Treacey

Stunt Co-ordinators
Jim Dowdall, Gareth Milne

Stunt Performer
Tracey Eddon

Insurance
Bayly, Martin & Fay International Ltd

Catering
The Good Eating Company

Nigel Terry
Michelangelo Caravaggio

Sean Bean
Ranuccio Thomasoni

Garry Cooper
Davide

Dexter Fletcher
young Caravaggio

Spencer Leigh
Jerusaleme

Tilda Swinton
Lena

Nigel Davenport
Giustiniani

Robbie Coltrane
Cardinal Scipione Borghese

Michael Gough
Cardinal Del Monte

Noam Almaz
Boy Caravaggio

Dawn Archibald
Pipo

Jack Birkett
Pope

Una Brandon-Jones
weeping woman

Imogen Claire
lady with the jewels

Sadie Corre
Princess Collona

Lol Coxhill
old priest

Vernon Dobtcheff
art lover

Terry Downes
bodyguard

Jonathan Hyde
Baglione

Emil Nicolau
young Jerusaleme

Gene October
model peeling fruit

Cindy Oswin
Lady Elizabeth

John Rogan
Vatican official

Zohra Segal
Jerusaleme's grandmother

Lucien Taylor
boy with guitar

Simon Turner
Fra Filippo

8,353 feet
93 minutes

In Colour